CRYING IN THE

CRYING IN THE WILDERNESS

David Smith

paternoster press

First published in 2000 by Paternoster Press

06 05 04 03 02 01 00   7 6 5 4 3 2 1

Paternoster Press is an imprint of Paternoster Publishing,
PO Box 300, Carlisle, Cumbria, CA3 0QS, UK
http://www.paternoster-publishing.com

British Library Cataloguing in Publication Data
A catalogue record for this book is available from the British Library

ISBN 0-85364-811-5

Cover Design by Mainstream, Lancaster
Typeset by WestKey Limited, Falmouth, Cornwall
Printed in Great Britain by Caledonian International
Book Manufacturing, Glasgow

This book is dedicated to

HOWEL JONES

*a true friend and brother without
whose constant encouragement it would
never have been published*

Contents

Introduction

Readers who are familiar with the Authorised Version of the Bible will realise that the title I have chosen for this book alludes to Matthew's description of the ministry of John the Baptist as fulfilling the prophecy of Isaiah: 'The voice of one *crying in the wilderness*, Prepare ye the way of the Lord, make his paths straight' (Mt. 3:3). My use of this phrase obviously involves a play on words in that I want to focus attention on both the tragedy of our cultural wilderness, the cries of anguish that can be heard coming from it, *and* the enormous challenge facing Christians who are committed to 'crying' in this wilderness, in the sense of proclaiming the good news of the Gospel in this context.

In respect of the first of these concerns, I want to encourage believers to listen with sympathy and compassion to the cries of pain and anguish that can be heard within our modern wilderness. To this end a major strand in the studies which make up this volume relates to the sense of alienation to which many contemporary people bear witness in modern, secular societies. Some of these voices belong to prominent and gifted people whose work, whether in academic, literary or artistic fields, is very well known. These are, I suggest, important witnesses and we do well to pay attention to the likes of Bertrand Russell, Albert Camus, Viktor Frankl, or to the legion of modern painters, novelists and musicians who have used the medium of the arts to give powerful expression to their awareness of the dilemmas and contradictions facing human beings today. Our libraries, art galleries, concert halls, theatres and movie houses, not to mention the vast arenas in which pop concerts take place, all of these echo to the voices of gifted people who express, often in unforgettable ways, the sadness, the sheer boredom, or at times the desperate rage of those for whom the wilderness is a place of tragic despair and death. Asked what he believed in, the American actor Woody Allen ruled out politics, science or religion and, with the pathos characteristic of the true comedian, declared, 'I believe in sex and death – two experiences that come once in a life-time.' Audiences may have laughed, but the laughter was surely checked by an awareness that such a hollowed-out creed is a fitting symbol for the weightlessness, the 'lightness of being', that is characteristic of contemporary life.

However, this *crying in the wilderness* can be heard far beyond the rather narrow confines of what may be called 'high culture'. Consider the tears shed among football supporters when the teams which provide functional substitutes for religion fail and the field of dreams loses its power to shield its devotees from despair. Or recall the crying which occurs when a celebrity (any celebrity) is exalted by the media into a secular saint and is then shown by the inexorable power of death to be mortal like the rest of us. Most of all, think of the simple and tragic grief of people, old and young, who suffer the social, economic and moral consequences of a culture which exalts *possessing* above *being* and knows of no foundation for ethics beyond the struggle for power and dominance. These are cries that must be heard by the followers of Jesus and must evoke in them, as they did in their saviour, a true compassion, a renewed commitment to truth and reality as these have been revealed in the Gospel, and a dedication to discipleship, service and mission within the wilderness of the modern world.

This brings me to the second central concern of this book: *crying* in the sense that is clearly intended in the text of the Authorised Version mentioned above – proclaiming a revolutionary and counter-cultural message of hope and liberation. The appearance of the Baptist in the wilderness and his announcement that the great Day of the Lord was about to dawn suggests that the wilderness, the place of marginality and struggle, is the one place where hope may be born and truly new beginnings are possible. The prophet in the desert may be despised by those who hold the reigns of power at the centre – as indeed was John the Baptist by the religious authorities in Jerusalem – but they cannot suppress the nagging fear that the evidently counter-cultural message being proclaimed there might actually pose a threat to the *status quo* if enough people begin to take it seriously. Preaching and prophecy, the effective and faithful communication of the Christian message, and a concern for the integrity of the churches – these are all aspects of the second major theme that readers will discover running through this book.

There is a further nuance to the word *crying* which, while not dealt with in this volume in any detailed way, must be mentioned here. If Christians must heed the tears of those lost in the wilderness, and if they are bound to imitate John the Baptist in crying 'Behold, the Lamb of God that takes away the sins of the world' in such a context, then I suggest that they will not themselves be strangers to tears. In this respect their true model is not the Baptist but the one to whom he pointed, the Christ who was 'a man of sorrows, acquainted with grief'. Alas, far too much Christian proclamation has been done by men with dry eyes. Looking out over a sea of tears such preachers have retained a dignified detachment which bears an uncanny likeness to the religious orthodoxy of the ecclesiastical police who descended on John the Baptist from Jerusalem. Preaching of this kind achieves nothing, except to further alienate the poor and needy and to confirm their impression that religious people are insufferable hypocrites whose self-righteousness marks them out as people to be avoided. Alan Flavelle once said that Evangelical churches too often convey the impression that being a Christian leaves a person with no unanswered questions, no nagging doubts, no unmastered sins. '*And the sham of it all stinks*! So often needy people are kept at a distance because we seem so self-assured . . . We need to tear off our masks, to let ourselves be seen as we really are – poor sinners living only by the grace of God.'

Crying in the wilderness then involves listening to and understanding those who weep in despair and rage, while bearing witness to the Christ who can transform our deserts into fruitful places and bring life out of death Yet this must be done with hearts that are moved by the tragedies of human lostness as well as by the awareness of personal failing and complete dependence on the grace that defies all logic, ignores all human calculations of worthiness and status, and leaves us speechless before the unfathomable love and kindness of the Father.

The chapters which make up this book originated as presentations and lectures in a number of different settings over the past ten years. Chapters One and Six were delivered as the Rigby Lectures at Northumbria Bible College in 1990 and 1998 respectively. They are printed here substantially as given then, although I have updated and modified them in some details. Chapters Two and Five are based on lectures given at the annual conference of the Scottish Evangelical Theological Society in Edinburgh and both appeared as articles in *Scottish Bulletin of Evangelical Theology*. Chapter Three also originated as a paper for the above-mentioned conference and it was published in a considerably modified form in the journal *Theology in Scotland*. I am grateful to the editors of both journals for permission to use this material here. Chapter Four began life at a Study Conference organised by the British Evangelical Council although it has been substantially rewritten for the purpose of publication in this volume.

Readers will notice that I have avoided the use of critical apparatus in this book and have made no attempt to supply detailed information about sources through footnotes or a detailed bibliography. The reason is simple: I wanted to avoid a formal academic style and to address as wide an audience as possible. My hope is that what is written here will be of help to thoughtful Christians, pastors and teachers, encouraging them to grapple with the cultural issues at the heart of mission in modern society and stimulating discussion on the nature and shape of the church in a post-Christendom era. While I shall of course be grateful if some of this material contributes to the developing scholarly discussion regarding the mission of the church in the third millennium, my main concern is to assist believers in facing the challenges posed to faith and discipleship today. Nonetheless, since I am bound to endeavour to acknowledge the sources from which I have learned so much, I have provided a 'Bibliographic Essay' in which every effort has been made to attribute the quotations used in the main text. My considerable debts to the books and articles listed there will be evident and I hope that readers wishing to pursue the study of the subject will find help and guidance in this section.

David Smith
Oxford,
Summer, 1999

One

A Tale of Two Centuries

'The missionary movement is now in its old age. It is not a useless or decrepit old age . . . But the conditions that produced the movement have changed, and they have been changed by the Lord of history. And the church has been changed out of all recognition by the agency of the missionary movement itself.'

Andrew Walls

In the spring of 1791 a young Baptist pastor named William Carey strongly urged fellow ministers meeting at Clipstone in Nottinghamshire that 'before they parted they would form a missionary society'. His brothers (not for the first time) declined to respond to Carey's passionate plea, but they did agree that a manuscript he had prepared on the subject of mission should be published. Consequently early in 1792 Carey's *Enquiry into the Obligations of Christians to Use Means for the Conversion of the Heathen* appeared in print. In October of that year Carey finally had his way when Baptist ministers, gathered at Kettering, agreed to subscribe from their own pockets in order to bring into being a missionary society. The sum collected amounted to £13-2s-6d – a total described at the time as 'sufficient for present purposes'.

Three aspects of the wider culture of the eighteenth century are significant in understanding the background to the birth of the modern missionary movement. *First*, this was *the age of discovery*. The world of the 1700s was at once much smaller and much larger than ours. It was smaller in the sense that geographical

knowledge extended only to patches of the inhabited globe. The
main outlines of the continents were known, but interior regions
were unexplored and the courses of the great rivers were matters
of speculation. At the same time, the world was infinitely vaster
than today on account of the slowness and uncertainty of communications. Even within the British Isles communications were
limited. When Charles Simeon, the Evangelical vicar of Holy
Trinity, Cambridge, visited Scotland the only way of returning to
the south was by purchasing 'a saddle horse at Stirling'. William
Carey, whose background was that of a rural artisan, had probably never seen the sea before sailing for India and it is unlikely that
he had travelled more than sixty miles from his home.

Travel between continents involved hazardous journeys by
ship in which the risk from violent weather or violent Frenchmen
was ever-present. News of Carey's safe arrival in India took more
than a year to filter back home. In this situation towns like Plymouth, Bristol and Liverpool became key centres since to be within
reach of a port was to be within reach of the world.

However, knowledge of the world was increasing rapidly. The
accounts of the voyages of Captain James Cook had immense
influence in the eighteenth century, providing new vistas of the
Pacific and its peoples. Carey was deeply interested in this new
knowledge. As a young man practising his trade as a shoemaker,
he read Cook's journals and devoured all the information he
could find about the new worlds now opening up. His friend
Andrew Fuller wrote that anyone visiting Carey in his shoemaker's workshop would discover 'a map of the world, with
sheets of paper pasted together, besmeared with shoemaker's
wax, and the moral state of every nation depicted with his pen'.

Secondly, Carey also lived in *an age of revolution*. The American Declaration of Independence was signed in 1776 and the
French Revolution cast its long shadow across Europe in 1789.
Within Britain the Industrial Revolution was underway, resulting
in massive social changes and the virtual collapse of traditional
ways of life. External changes were accompanied by a growth of
radical ideas in religion and politics. The overlap between the
early missionary movement and this broad context is illustrated

by the fact that the London publisher of Carey's *Enquiry*, Joseph Johnson, also published Tom Paine's *The Rights of Man* and Mary Wollstonecraft's *Vindication of the Rights of Women*. Indeed, it was in Johnson's home that William Blake is said to have warned Paine to flee to Paris in 1792.

In later years Baptist missionaries in India went out of their way to distance themselves from expatriates sympathetic to Paine's political radicalism. In the 1790s however, Carey and his friends walked a political tightrope at a time when the defenders of the *status quo* were gripped by a paranoid fear of the appearance of revolutionary groups in Britain. In this atmosphere the formation of a 'voluntary society' was a hazardous business, especially when undertaken by Baptist Dissenters who had been under suspicion since their republican sympathies had been evident when King Charles lost his head. Sydney Smith, an inveterate opponent of missions, was quite explicit in warning that the spread of Evangelicalism bore sinister parallels with what he called 'the last great eruption of fanaticism' a century and half earlier which, he said, had 'destroyed both Church and Throne with its tremendous force'.

Mention of 'Evangelicalism' reminds us of the *third* major factor in the shaping of eighteenth-century culture, *the revival movement known as the 'Great Awakening'*. The missionary impulse which finally received institutional expression in the 1790s can be traced to the transformation in the theology and spirituality of much of British Christianity as a result of the revival. When Thomas Coke, who is rightly called the father of Methodist overseas missions, was ejected from his living in Somerset in 1776, he asked John Wesley what he should do without parish or church? 'Why,' Wesley replied, 'go and preach the Gospel to all the world.' Coke took these words seriously and in 1783, fully eight years before Carey's *Enquiry* appeared, he published a detailed proposal for the establishment of a Methodist missionary society. Although Coke's plan was not adopted at the time, it illustrates the missionary impulse released by the Great Awakening. The global range of the Evangelical vision is perfectly reflected in Charles Wesley's lines:

O that the world might taste and see
The riches of his grace,
The arms of love that compass me
Would all mankind embrace.

Missionary work has come to be regarded as so characteristic of Protestant Christianity that we may easily overlook the radically innovative nature of the step taken by Carey and his friends. In fact, Roman Catholics had often pointed out the failure of the Reformers and their successors to engage in mission. Cardinal Bellarmine observed that although the Lutherans compared themselves to the apostles, they were decidedly unapostolic when it came to preaching to the heathen. Some Protestants reacted to this Catholic polemic with the argument that Christ had never intended mission to be an abiding mark of the church. Johann Gerhard, for example, taught that the Great Commission had been given exclusively to the apostles. This view was not uncommon among seventeenth-century Protestants.

To their great credit, the Anabaptists, the people of the so-called Radical Reformation, developed a view of mission close to that found on the pages of the New Testament. Challenging the entire concept of Christendom they insisted that the church consists of believers called out of the world and gathered together in a community marked by conscious, personal faith. Anabaptist evangelists criss-crossed Europe seeking converts and paid a terrible price in suffering and death, yet modern Christianity acknowledges its debt to them for their courageous advocacy of the principle of religious liberty, and their awareness that mission is part of the nature of the church.

By Carey's time, many Baptists in England had become ensnared in a rigidly deterministic Calvinism which made consideration of the church's missionary obligation impossible. This rationalist form of hyper-Calvinism, which was accompanied by a highly introverted piety, led to complete inertia as far as preaching to the wider world was concerned. The theologian most representative of this tradition was John Gill. Responding to the lament of the Welsh preacher, Christmas Evans, that Gill's works had never been translated into his native tongue, the great Baptist preacher Robert Hall said, 'I wish they had, sir . . . for then, I should never had read them! They are a continent of mud sir!'

How then did the modern missionary movement emerge from such a background? How did Carey escape from a theological 'continent of mud' to argue with such conviction and passion that Christians must 'use means' to convert the unevangelized?

On the one hand, William Carey was profoundly stirred and challenged by the widening horizons of his generation. As we have already seen, his friends spoke of his inexhaustible thirst for geographical knowledge. From the time of his ordination as a Baptist pastor, it was said that he never met fellow ministers without conversing with them 'on the importance and practicability of missions'. The mainspring of Carey's missionary passion is to be found in his interpretation of Scripture and, in particular, in the way in which he and his contemporaries understood biblical prophecy. At the very beginning of his *Enquiry* Carey asserted that God had 'repeatedly made known his intention to prevail finally over all the power of the Devil . . . and to set up his own kingdom among men, and extend it as universally as Satan had extended his'. Eighteenth-century Evangelicals possessed an inexhaustible confidence in the power of the grace of God and believed that they stood on the brink of a time when the Gospel of Christ was destined to renew and transform the whole of the earth. This belief had been given classic expression earlier in the century in the words of Isaac Watts' hymn:

> Jesus shall reign where'er the sun
> Doth his successive journeys run,
> His kingdom stretch from shore to shore,
> Till moons shall wax and wane no more.

By Carey's time, it seemed as though history was confirming the imminence of this age of millennial glory: Cook's discoveries in the Pacific, recent events in America, and even the Revolution in France were, in his view, events pregnant with spiritual

significance. Carey was deeply influenced by the American theologian Jonathan Edwards and agreed with him that a time was
coming when 'true Christianity shall in every respect be upper-
most in the world'. In later years we hear echoes of this belief
again and again in the reports sent back from India. The hope that
the Gospel was destined to triumph across the world not only
inspired the founding of the mission, but sustained it in the face of
setbacks and disappointments. Carey's most famous statement,
derived from the headings of the sermon preached in Nottingham
in 1792, takes us to the heart of his missionary conviction:
'Expect great things from God; attempt great things for God.'

Of particular interest is the manner in which the first Baptist
missionaries related to the cultures and religions of the East.
Some of the earliest missionary reports from India inform friends
at home that the Hindus were remarkably gentle and tolerant
people. Carey's close colleague John Thomas wrote that Indians
were 'distinguished from all people on the face of the earth for
their harmless and inoffensive behaviour'. Later, when William
Ward's ship was approaching Calcutta, he expressed delight at
the prospect of spending his life with these 'gentle and placid'
people and said that his desire was to be 'a converted Hindoo'.
No trace of racial superiority can be found in these missionaries;
indeed, they went out of their way to recognise whatever was
noble and good in the culture of their hearers. This is not to say
that they ignored the darker side of Indian culture; when they
encountered practices which appeared to violate the fundamental moral law of God they were not slow to protest at such
things. Carey first witnessed a widow being burned on the
funeral pyre of her husband in 1799 and warned those present
that he would certainly bear witness to what he had seen at the
tribunal of God! At the same time Carey and his friends wrestled
with the languages of India, read many of the sacred books of
Hinduism and Confucianism, and even published English trans-
lations of some of the sacred books of the East on the press at
Serampore. New missionaries were advised that obtaining deep
insight into Indian culture was an absolute prerequisite to effective witness and mission on the subcontinent. Thus, William

Ward urged a missionary candidate in 1821 to obtain from Hindus 'an account of their religion; its theory, ceremonies, etc. Statements made by themselves will be more correct than what you can find in books; and in gaining the relation from one on whom the system has made a strong impression, you will find matter for thought, for sermons, and for prayer, which you could obtain by no other process.'

So marked was this sensitivity to Indian culture that questions were asked at home as to just what the missionaries were up to! What was Carey doing printing the Hindu epic, the *Mahabharata*, and the works of Confucius on a Baptist press? The fact is that the missionaries were determined that Indian churches planted through their witness should reflect the Asian cultural context in every way possible. Their policy was, in William Ward's words, 'to make India evangelize itself and all the surrounding regions'. To this end, he said, 'we have carefully avoided everything which might Anglicise the converts. We have made no changes in their dress, their names, their food, their language, or their domestic habits.' He took pride in pointing out that the first Indian convert, Krishna Pal, baptised twenty years earlier, appeared among his countrymen 'as much a Hindu as ever, those things contrary to Christianity excepted'. This deep concern to ensure that converts should not be cut adrift from Indian culture was reflected in the structure of the curriculum at Serampore College which was designed to teach Christianity within the context of Indian religion and culture. Joshua Marshman articulated the missionaries' vision of an India transformed by the Gospel when he expressed the hope that it would become a land 'Christian but still essentially Indian' in which 'the oriental classics shall be cultivated in subservience to divine revelation, and when the splendid imagery of the great national poets shall be employed to elucidate and adorn Christian truth'.

Another remarkable characteristic of the earliest Baptist missionaries concerns their extraordinary devotion to their task. Soon after arriving in India Carey wrote, 'What is there in all this world worth living for, but the presence and service of God? I feel a burning desire that all the world may know this God and serve

him. Oh! how long will it be ere I shall know so much of the language as to preach Christ crucified in it!' In the following years the
enterprise suffered many setbacks and disappointments. The
early hope of the rapid spread of Christianity in India was frus-
trated; the ancient walls of Hinduism did not crumble before the
sound of the Gospel trumpets, nor did the eagerly anticipated millennial glory break forth across the world. By 1821 William Ward
confessed that 'The restricted progress of Christianity and the
moral darkness in which so great a portion of the globe has
remained . . . forms one of the most mysterious dispensations of
Providence which has ever occupied human attention.' Added to
this, the missionary family suffered a series of calamities and
bereavements which might easily have crushed their spirits
and destroyed their hopes. In 1801 William Ward, sitting through
the night beside a dying colleague, wrote, 'Our love to one
another grows exceedingly and every new death makes us cling
the closer.' The Serampore missionaries stuck to their task with a
persistence, dedication and undiminished hopefulness which is
astonishing. Bound together in an apostolic form of communism,
they signed a document each year which contained these words:
'Let us give ourselves up unreservedly to this glorious cause. Let
us never think that our time, our gifts, our strength, our families,
or even the clothes we wear, are our own.'

In the course of the nineteenth century the missionary movement grew in size and was changed in character. Having begun
under a cloud of suspicion, it emerged into respectability to
become a recognised part of Victorian culture. In 1791 Carey
could be dismissed as a 'Baptist cobbler' and his calling as a missionary challenged as dangerous to British interests in India; a
century later we discover a missionary, in the person of the great
David Livingstone, as a culture-hero of the Empire. This transformation reflected the massive growth of evangelical influence
within British Christianity, a growth which has led one recent historian to describe the hundred years prior to the First World War
as 'the Evangelical century'. However, numerical increase and
social respectability have negative as well as positive consequences. Every year thousands of middle-class Evangelicals

congregated in London for the annual missionary meetings at the
Exeter Hall in the Strand. These gatherings, known as the 'May
Meetings', became great social events and the satirical magazine
Punch was not slow to poke fun at them. Thus, in May 1856 the
following piece of doggerel appeared in its pages:

> 'Tis the sweet month of May love; the saints are all gay love
> Though they flee from the play love, the opera and ball,
> Then, as this is our season, dost thou know any reason
> That should hinder our meeting at Exeter Hall?
> Be thou sure to be there love, and I will repair love,
> To the portals right early thy coming to bide,
> In order to find thee, and sit close behind thee,
> If I may not attain to a seat by thy side.
>
> Ah! say thou'lt comply love, nay do not deny love!
> For grief I shall cry love in case thou refuse.
> What day shall we go love? There are many you know love:
> City missions, or Pastoral Aid, or the Jews?
> All alike will be pleasant, if thou art but present;
> Each in turn will afford something certain to please,
> From a tale of excursion for Irish conversion,
> To a preacher's experiences among the Feejees.

We are bound to ask whether this satirical attack on missions
suggests that the evangelical vision of the goal of cross-cultural
witness had shrunk? What happened to Carey's hope that the
whole world was about to be transformed by the spread of
the Gospel? While Carey and his colleagues certainly did not
preach a 'social Gospel' and were not overtly political in their
missionary aims, they did believe that mission would produce a
profound change in the structure of Indian society. For them, the
conversion of individuals to Christ was certainly a missiological
priority, yet their aims extended beyond the saving of souls to
include no less than the transformation of the Indian worldview.
In 1810 Ward wrote that the signs of the times pointed to
the arrival of 'glorious days' when the remaining obstacles to the

Gospel in India would be removed and thousands would enjoy the blessings of the kingdom of Jesus and what he called 'the new shastra of the Gospel'.

This understanding of the purposes of God in sending the church into the world persisted well into the nineteenth century and continued to be held by some very prominent Evangelicals. For example, the great Baptist preacher Charles Haddon Spurgeon told the annual meeting of the Baptist Missionary Society in 1858 that the Gospel would one day so transform society as to make the very name of war intolerable. Spurgeon insisted that the Bible taught 'that when the Gospel has its day, wars must cease to the ends of the earth'. However, by this time a different view of the prospects for the Gospel had gained ground among Evangelicals and Spurgeon's confidence was not shared by many of his contemporaries. A growing number of Evangelicals had come to believe that biblical prophecy pointed not to the renewal and transformation of this world, but to its irreversible decay and imminent destruction. Among those responsible for this changed emphasis was John Nelson Darby, founder of the movement later to be known as the Plymouth Brethren. Lecturing in Geneva in 1840, Darby poured scorn on the old idea that Christians might expect mission to result in a 'progress of good' in the world. Such hope, Darby said, was delusive since a proper reading of prophecy leads to the conclusion that all we can expect within history is a 'progress of evil'.

This profoundly negative view of the world had inevitable implications for mission; the social dimension of witness receded as emphasis was increasingly placed on rescuing individuals from a world for which no hope could be entertained. What might be called a 'lifeboat' model of mission became influential, a concept explicitly endorsed by the American evangelist D.L. Moody who described the world as 'a wrecked vessel' and said that God had given him a lifeboat with the commission to 'save all you can'. The hymns of Wesley and Watts, so full of confidence in the transformative power of the grace of God, were increasingly replaced by a new type of song, of which Philip Bliss' lines are typical:

> Ho my comrades! see the signal
> Waving in the sky!
> Reinforcements now appearing,
> Victory is nigh!
> Hold the fort for I am coming
> Jesus signals still
> Wave the answer back to heaven
> By thy grace we will.

By 1891 then, a significant section of the Evangelical movement seemed to be engaged in retreat before the forces of the modern world. For such Evangelicals, what the Gospel might be expected to achieve within history was severely limited; their task was to defend an outpost stranded in enemy territory until the glorious Second Advent of Christ.

What of the situation at the close of the twentieth century? I want to suggest that there are remarkable parallels between our times and those of William Carey. Carey's age was one of change and social crisis; so is ours. He lived at a point at which old theological systems were exhausted and discredited; so do we. The early Baptist missionaries had to confront a culture marked by religious pluralism and were compelled to come to terms with the task of planting the church in such an environment; we face a similar challenge.

In particular, I suggest there are three crucial factors which must be taken into account as we think about mission 'today and tomorrow'. Professor Andrew Walls has said, 'Not long ago Christianity was the religion of nearly all the peoples of Europe and of their New World descendants, and of few others. Today it is a faith distributed throughout the world, is especially characteristic of the Southern continents and appears to be receding only among the peoples of European origin.' In the eighteenth century, Jonathan Edwards made the unlikely suggestion that the time was not far off when outstanding theologians would come from black Africa. That remarkable prophecy is now being fulfilled as new centres of dynamic theological reflection are emerging in many parts of the non-Western world. If Carey, Marshman and Ward were present today they would feel that in many respects their vision of the spread of the Gospel in Africa, Asia and Latin America has become a reality. At any rate, the spiritual centre of gravity in world Christianity has shifted decisively from the north to the south of the globe and it will no longer do to sing as though all the heathens dwell in darkness 'far, far away'.

If the growth of churches in the non-Western world is one crucial factor which shapes mission at the dawn of the third millennium, the second distinguishing element in our situation concerns the challenge of resurgent religions. By the year 1891 it was widely believed that the ancient religious traditions of peoples outside Europe were facing decline and extinction. This belief rested in large part on an evolutionary understanding of the history of religion; Europe stood at the pinnacle of historical progress while 'savages' elsewhere belonged to an earlier phase in the evolution of the human race. Western civilisation and culture represented, so it was believed, the very goal of history and were destined to lead the whole world in their triumphant march. At the annual meetings of the Baptist Missionary Society in 1898, G.C. Lorrimer said that 'the united energies, faith and wealth of Great Britain and the United States . . . should be able in a few years to conquer heathen darkness . . .' He spoke about the 'flags of the two living nations' blending together as, bathed in the splendour of the Cross of Christ, they 'move across the globe'. This was a form of culture-religion utterly remote from the faith of William Carey. However, as our century has unfolded, Hinduism, Buddhism and Islam have refused to accept their position in the evolutionary scheme and, far from declining and dying, have undergone remarkable transformations and revivals. According to one researcher there are today over 817 million Muslims in the world, a figure likely to rise to 1,200 million by the end of the century. Writing about the non-Christian religions the Dutch missionary theologian Hendrik Kraemer observed, 'A century ago we could ignore their existence. They seemed immaterial to the dominating curve of history so patently embodied in the western world. Today it is impossible to ignore them; and their development, good or evil, will affect all other parts of the world.'

As we face this challenge in mission we have much to learn from Carey. We need both his sensitivity to other cultures and his consuming passion to communicate the message of Christ to those beyond the reach of normal missionary work. In 1793, with one son seriously ill, Carey wrote, 'I had fully intended to devote my eldest son to the study of Sanscrit, my second to Persian, and my third to Chinese . . . if God should hereafter bless them with his grace, this may fit them for a mission in any part of Persia, India or China.'

Finally, the most obvious contrast between our situation today and the world of either 1791 or 1891 concerns the decay of Western culture. Outwardly and materially, the West remains relatively strong and prosperous, yet morally and spiritually there is growing awareness of a terrifying emptiness and lostness. Science and technology, hailed as saviours in 1891, now appear as, at best, mixed blessings. The optimism so evident then has been replaced by a brooding sense of the ultimate meaninglessness of life in a godless world. We lack any firm basis for morality and seem to be prey to a host of bizarre beliefs and cruel idols. The temptations facing the churches in this situation are either to take flight into the past, ignoring the real needs of this age, or to accept that their function is merely to provide peace and assurance to individuals, so opting out of the challenge of mission to a post-Christian society which, according to many secular analysts, is in deepening crisis.

In relation to each of the three aspects of the missionary challenge confronting us today, the father of the modern missionary movement can challenge, inspire and guide us. In 1794, just over a year after arriving in India, William Carey wrote, 'When I first left England my hope of the conversion of the heathen was very strong, but among so many obstacles it would utterly die away unless upheld by God . . . I have no earthly thing to depend upon. Well, I have God, and his word is sure; and though the superstitions of the heathen were a million times more deeply rooted, and the examples of Europeans a million times worse than they are, if I were deserted by all and persecuted by all, yet my hope, fixed on that sure word, will rise superior to all obstructions, and triumph over all trials; God's cause will triumph, and I shall come out of all trials as gold purified in the fire.'

Could we possibly find a better missionary model than this for the new millennium?

Two

Doing Theology in the Wilderness

'Unless the church in the West begins [to] develop a missionary theology, not just a theology of mission, we will not achieve more than merely a patch up of the church. We are in need of a missiological agenda for theology, not just a theological agenda for mission . . .'

David Bosch

In 1965 I completed a three-year course in theology and began pastoral ministry in the university city of Cambridge. I have many reasons to be thankful for my training, not least because it convinced me of the central importance of expository preaching and gave me an excellent biblical foundation for such a ministry. However, in one area in particular my studies seemed sadly deficient; mission was absolutely marginal within the course, confined to occasional visits by people called, rather curiously, 'missionary statesmen'.

Recently I came across some words of the Scottish missionary thinker Alexander Duff in which, reflecting on his preparation for ministry, he identified similar weaknesses in theological education in nineteenth-century Britain. Like me, Duff was profoundly grateful for the blessings he experienced at his Alma Mater; it was said that he could never speak of Saint Andrew's 'except in terms approaching sheer rhapsody'. However, addressing the General Assembly of the Free Church of Scotland in 1867 on the occasion of his election to the newly-created chair of Evangelistic Theology, Duff noted one glaring omission from the theological curriculum during his student days:

I was struck markedly with this circumstance, that throughout the whole course of the curriculum of four years not one single allusion was ever made to the subject of the world's evangelisation – the subject which constitutes the chief end of the Christian Church on earth. I felt intensely that there was something wrong with this omission. According to any just conception of the Church of Christ, the grand function it has to discharge in this world cannot be said to begin and end in the preservation of internal purity of doctrine, discipline and government. All this is merely for burnishing it so as to be a lamp to give light not to itself only but also to the world. There must be an outcome of that light, lest it prove useless, and thereby be lost and extinguished. Why has it got that light, but that it should freely impart it to others?

The professorship to which Duff was inducted after this speech was intended to remedy the neglect of mission studies in the theological curriculum. It was the first chair of Mission in Europe and represented a bold and innovative step in theological education. Sadly the experiment scarcely survived Duff's death in 1878 and mission studies has had a difficult time finding a home in the theological faculty ever since.

However, as we face the wilderness of modern culture the question of the relationship between theology and mission has become urgent and unavoidable. Theological study on a traditional Western model faces a crisis of confidence. Among the many voices raised in protest against traditional patterns of theological education, we may note the words of a former Archbishop of Canterbury. Present patterns of training, according to Robert Runcie, 'are either too academic or too influenced by university models'. At the same time, the traditional Western approach to theological education has been widely rejected elsewhere in the world. Around the globe voices are raised against an approach to theology that is perceived to be too academic, too abstract, and too remote from the actual tasks of mission and witness in a religiously plural world. John Mbiti has observed that the curricula used in theological seminaries in Africa showed them to be 'very much out of touch with the realities of African culture and problems'. Mbiti asked:

Have we not enough musical instruments to raise the thunderous sound of the glory of God even unto the heaven of heavens? Have we not enough mouths to sing the rhythms of the Gospel in our tunes until it settles in our bloodstream? Have we not hearts in this continent, to contemplate the marvels of the Christian faith? ... Have we not enough intellectuals in this continent to reflect and theologise on the meaning of the Gospel? Have we not enough feet on this continent, to carry the Gospel to every corner of this globe?

Mbiti's words clearly imply that Christian theology developed in Africa will be inextricably bound up with mission. Indeed, they underline the point made in the previous chapter that a fundamental shift has occurred by means of which the real centres of spiritual vitality and missionary expansion are now located in the southern hemisphere. Consciousness of this change is widespread in the Third World and theologians in Africa, Latin America and Asia increasingly ask whether the churches in the West have yet woken up to the reality of this new era in Christian mission. For example, Choan-Seng Song notes that predictions concerning the growth of the Christian population in Asia, Africa, Oceania and South America, will mean that believers in the West will need to ask themselves some heart-searching questions:

What will the future of Christianity be in their own lands? How are they going to recapture the power of the gospel, especially in those countries where there is increasing indifference to the church? And how are they going to relate to Christians in the Third World who will surpass them in numerical strength?

This statement by an Asian theologian leads directly to another factor which compels us to place the subject of mission at the top of the theological agenda today. When Duff spoke in 1867, very few of his contemporaries discerned the forces at work within the Victorian age which were even then beginning to undermine faith and were to result in the radical secularization of British culture. So far as they were concerned, mission was something done on a distant shore, among peoples unfortunate enough to live beyond

the sphere of Christendom in lands benighted by the influence of
'paganism'. Today the picture has changed completely; Christianity has ceased to be a European phenomenon and has become a
world faith. Speaking of this development, Andrew Walls
comments that signs of Christianity's decline in Europe became
evident 'just as it was expanding everywhere else'. This decline of
faith in Europe has led to a situation in which a leading Christian
thinker can argue that the most urgent missiological question
today is whether the West can be converted. In this situation
mission studies, so long left homeless, must be admitted to the
seminary, not as a condescending act of compassion, but because
this excluded and marginalized subject may be capable of revital-
ising theology and offering the Western church a way to genuine
renewal.

In a series of writings the late David Bosch helpfully surveyed
the history of theological reflection on the Christian mission and
identified a series of historical paradigms which have shaped the
church's understanding of its missionary calling throughout
the centuries. In the earliest phase, Bosch notes, mission appears
to have been the natural expression of the life of the church. Witness to the world through words and deeds which reflect the truth
and values of the kingdom of God was not something debated or
discussed. Rather, Christians lived as strangers and pilgrims in an
alien world and took it for granted that they were called to act as
salt and light. In a context of cultural and religious pluralism mission was neither an option nor a duty, but simply an integral part
of what it meant to be Christian. It might be said that the church
in this period was scarcely conscious of its own identity;
ecclesiology is of little interest in periods of revival and missionary
advance since the absorbing interest is christology and life
becomes a doxology.

David Bosch regarded the conversion of Constantine as the
crucial turning point in the church's perception of its role within
the world. Growing institutionalisation removed the sense of
being a pilgrim people and mission became equated with church
extension. For well over a thousand years mission was to be
understood in relation to the *Corpus Christianum*. Bosch suggests

that the Middle Ages witnessed the emergence of an attitude of religious and cultural superiority to those outside Christendom which was to persist into the present century. Indeed, it is impossible to exaggerate the extent to which the ideology of Christendom influenced the churches in Europe. Even today, amid the ruins of past ecclesiastical power, the mentality of the *Corpus Christianum* clings to us in all kinds of ways and continues to shape our thinking about mission.

However, within the last hundred years mission studies (or, as our American friends prefer, missiology) has made its appearance and has sought entry to the divinity faculty. This very fact reflects a deepening awareness that the challenge of the task confronting the church in a pluralist world requires serious biblical and theological reflection on the nature of mission. As Bosch says, 'the Christian church in general and the Christian mission in particular are today confronted by issues which they have never even dreamt of and which are crying out for responses which are both relevant to the times and in harmony with the essence of the Christian faith'.

If the need for theological reflection on the task of mission in the modern world is increasingly recognised, there is no consensus as to how this laudable objective might be achieved. Traditionally the theological curriculum has been divided into three or four major subject areas: Biblical studies, dogmatics, and historical studies have formed the indispensable core of divinity courses, with practical (or pastoral) studies having been added during the nineteenth century. It is not clear how these subject areas relate to each other, nor is it obvious how additional subjects (worship, for instance, or ethics) might find a place in such a system. Moreover, the approach to theological studies has tended to be highly academic. Colin Chapman has likened traditional courses in divinity to the first two years of pre-clinical medicine, with the critical study of the Bible, dogmatics, and Western church history being comparable to courses in the basic sciences, anatomy and physiology. Introducing mission studies into this setting would seem to have as little hope of success as asking an order of monks committed to silence to accommodate an extreme charismatic.

Perhaps the crucial question is that posed by David Bosch: whether we need a theology of mission or, more radically, a missionary theology? Of course one must be thankful that increasing attention is being given today to the theology of mission. In North America 'Schools of World Mission' have been founded in many leading seminaries and missiology is a high-profile subject. American missiologists such as Eugene Nida, Charles Kraft, Harvie Conn, and David Hesselgrave have produced work of very high quality and have offered considerable assistance to men and women called to communicate the message of the Gospel across cultural boundaries. However, the great disadvantage of this approach is that it leaves the study of mission isolated from the rest of the theological curriculum, perpetuating the impression that this is, after all, an optional concern likely to be pursued by enthusiasts. Worse still, this approach inoculates theological studies as such against the challenge and disturbance that will inevitably occur when missiological questions begin to be raised at the heart of the divinity school. Doubtless missiologists, who are inclined to employ insights from the social sciences in order to suggest more effective methodologies in cross-cultural communication, do need to listen to the questions raised by theologians; but equally, given the condition of the world at the close of the twentieth century, theology simply cannot be done today without reference to the new era of world mission in which we find ourselves.

As long ago as 1948 H.P. van Dusen delivered a lecture in Illinois in which he demanded that mission studies be given centre stage in theological education. His words have a prophetic ring to them and they are worth quoting at some length:

Christian mission, which now holds an incidental and precarious position in so many seminary curricula, an addendum to the main subject matter, should move to a place of unchallenged centrality. It should be presented as the key to Church History, the seedplot of Christian Ecumenics, and the growing edge of Christianity's most vigorous and vital impact on the world of today and tomorrow, making far more urgent demand upon our attention and our devotion than

homiletics, pastoral theology, religious education, or any of the other
traditional instruments of perpetuating our familiar parish activities.

Van Dusen's passionate plea leads us to consider what a genuinely
missionary theology might look like. What might be the practical
implications of allowing missiological objectives to shape the
subject areas of theological studies and training for Christian
ministry and leadership today?

It scarcely needs to be said that Biblical Studies would be
released from captivity to an arid, purely technical approach to
the text of Scripture. Such an approach, says Walter Wink, is
bankrupt simply because it is incapable of making the Bible come
alive so as 'to illumine our present with new possibilities for personal and social transformation'. By contrast, a missiological
reading of the biblical text would reveal how the witnessing
activity of the church is founded upon the *missio Dei* and would
shed new light on the manner in which all Scripture is useful in
equipping the man of God 'for every good work' (2 Tim. 3:16).
For example, I simply do not know how to avoid the missionary
implications of the Song of Songs in a culture which has forgot-
ten the meaning of pure love. Stanley Hauerwas and William
Willimon have made the penetrating observation that when
orgasm has become one of the few contemporary routes to
self-transcendence 'Christians are going to have a tough time
convincing people that it would be nicer if they would not be
promiscuous'. In this context of cultural wilderness the 'lessons
in loving' offered by this inspired Hebrew poet are of far more
than academic interest. In the same manner, the apologetic value
of Ecclesiastes in an age of nihilism, or the message of Job in a
century that has witnessed the sufferings of Auschwitz and
Belsen, or the deep questioning and anguished wrestling with
God that one finds in the book of Psalms, all of this is pregnant
with potential for a missionary church at the dawn of the third
millennium. We have said nothing of the message of the prophets
or the parables of Jesus, nor has mention been made of the
visions of the Apocalypse, so crucial to a genuinely Christian
analysis of our times and so vital to believers' self-understanding

in a secularised and materialistic culture. Clearly, when read missiologically, the Bible places spiritual dynamite in our hands.

Of course, such a reading of the Bible requires an openness to interpretations of the text from brothers and sisters who read scripture from socio-cultural contexts different from ours. Let me cite just one example. Jeremiah's assault on a form of religion that had, in reality, become an ideology justifying and defending evil practices is illumined by Kosuke Koyama's book *Mount Fuji and Mount Sinai*. Here is a Japanese Christian attempting to understand what happened to his country and his people and dis-covering exact parallels between the temple liturgy denounced by the biblical prophet and the cult of the emperor in pre-war Japan. I now ask students to read Koyama as a modern inter-preter of Jeremiah's temple sermon (Jeremiah 7: 1–29; 26: 1–24) and then to reflect on the continuing danger posed by religious ideologies of various kinds in the modern world.

In a similar way, opening up dogmatic theology to missiological perspectives and questions offers exciting possibili-ties for the revitalisation of the subject. Bosch asks the question, 'How can so much of systematic theology remain blind and deaf to the fact that the total situation of the Christian church in the West and elsewhere is today a missionary one?' He quotes Martin Kahler as saying that theology is a 'companion of the Christian mission . . . not a luxury of the world-dominating church'. The work of the late Lesslie Newbigin was refreshing and stimulating, I suggest, precisely because it offered a missiological response to modern culture. Commenting on the inadequacy of the North American approach to mission, Newbigin observed that while missiological writing in the United States had endeavoured to explore the problems of contextualization in the cultures of humankind from China to Peru, 'it has largely ignored the culture that is the most widespread, powerful and persuasive among all contemporary cultures – namely . . . modern Western culture'. In actual fact, according to Newbigin, 'there is no higher priority for the research work of missiologists than to ask the question of what would be involved in a genuinely missionary encounter between the gospel and this modern Western culture'.

I would want to change only one word in this statement, replacing the American term 'missiologists' with the word 'theologians'. The encounter between the Gospel and post-modern culture for which Newbigin so eloquently pleads is surely a task so absolutely vital, yet so demanding and difficult, that it should be at the top of the agenda of every theological faculty and seminary.

However, it is important to add that this focus on the missionary challenge of the West, vital though it undoubtedly is, should not blind us to the truly ecumenical dimensions of a genuinely missionary theology. We have a greater opportunity now than at any previous point in Christian history to discover the width, length, height and depth of the love of Christ 'together with all the saints' (Eph. 3:17). Indeed, theology will be better equipped to meet the challenge of mission in the West if it draws upon the insights into the meaning of the Gospel provided by the churches of the Southern hemisphere.

Finally, what about the third main subject area of traditional theological studies, Church History? What would be involved in looking at the history of Christian expansion over the centuries from the perspective of mission? Andrew Walls, who has thought deeply on this matter over many years, suggests that 'the whole history of the church belongs to the whole church'. He writes, 'The global transformation of Christianity requires nothing less than the complete rethinking of the church history syllabus.' Here once again, the history of the expansion of Christianity across cultures during the past centuries is of enormous relevance to the missiological task now facing the church in the modern West. Moreover, the study of the history of the first evangelisation of Europe is pregnant with lessons of vital importance to a church which now faces the challenge of the re-evangelisation of the continent. For eight years in the 1990s as I walked to work at Northumbria Bible College, I caught a glimpse of the island of Lindisfarne along the coast. I am more and more struck by the fact that the missionary movement once centred on that island is not just of antiquarian interest, but offers examples and principles that are of great practical value in relation to our task today.

Emil Brunner once famously suggested that the church lives by mission as a flame lives by burning. If we take Brunner's words seriously and recognise that mission belongs to the very essence and nature of the church, then we are surely bound to conclude that we need not merely a theology of mission, but a missionary theology. We simply cannot afford the luxury of regarding mission as an addendum, something added to the existing curriculum in order to guarantee respectability. In a post-Christendom, pluralist world, we must recover the apostolic understanding of the church and its calling and recognize mission as inseparable from a life of obedience to Jesus as Lord. Only then will the church in the modern West rediscover its true nature and identity, recognising that it 'can never in any respect be an end in itself' but that 'it exists only as it exercises the ministry of a herald'. As Karl Barth puts it, 'Its mission is not additional to its being. It is, as it is sent and active in its mission. It builds itself up for the sake of its mission and in relation to it.' In such a church, theology and mission become indistinguishable.

Three

Mapping the Wilderness –
Modern Scotland as a Case Study

'Christianity has arrived at the end of its sojourn as the official, or established, religion of the Western world.'

Douglas John Hall

There are a variety of ways in which we can gain an understanding of the culture of a particular nation or people. In relation to modern societies one source of information is what is called public art: monuments, public buildings, statues. The statues erected in Edinburgh tell a very interesting story in relation to the history and culture of Scotland. The monument which dominates the centre of the city is that which houses the statue of Sir Walter Scott beside Princes Street. Close by there is a much smaller statue commemorating the great nineteenth-century Christian missionary, David Livingstone, whom we encountered earlier in this book. Glasgow also has a statue of Livingstone, and his birthplace at Blantyre has functioned as a Scottish National Memorial since 1925. A few hundred yards from the Livingstone statue in Princes Street there are statues of two outstanding Evangelical preachers – Thomas Guthrie and, looking down from George Street, Thomas Chalmers. From this vantage point it is possible to look across to New College on the Mound, knowing that just inside the entrance there is to be found a huge statue of another Protestant preacher, the reformer John Knox. It is doubtful whether there is another city in the world in which public art reflects the impact of Evangelical religion on national history and culture in such a remarkable way.

Consider the contrast with London. I am not aware of any monument erected there in public space to honour a missionary or an Evangelical preacher. The best known statue in London is that of Lord Nelson and the capital is dotted with the figures of past political and, especially, military heroes. In recent years the appearance of Whitehall has been changed by the erection of a series of statues and busts commemorating modern military leaders and the Strand now hosts the controversial statue of 'Bomber' Harris.

We have already had reason to notice the views of the great Victorian preacher C.H. Spurgeon on the subject of war so it may not be surprising to discover his reaction to the erection of the statues of military leaders in London. Preaching for the Baptist Missionary Society in 1857, Spurgeon denounced such statues as 'the trickery of an ignorant age, the gewgaws of a people that loved bloodshed despite their profession of religion'. Spurgeon anticipated the time when Nelson will be pulled down from his column and replaced by a statue of George Whitefield and the iron and brass of every statue standing in the city will be sold 'and the price thereof cast at the apostles' feet, that they may make distribution as every man hath need'.

But to return to Edinburgh. Our search for the distinctive features of Scottish culture might take us inside the National Gallery where, among some wonderful Scottish paintings, we find J.H. Lorimer's work *Ordination of Elders*. This picture, which captures the moment at which local worthies are inducted into office by the minister of the kirk, offers a further indicator of the significance of Protestant Christianity in Scotland. More specifically, it points to the influence of Presbyterianism and Calvinism and again reminds us of the role of the Bible in this culture. John Philip's painting *Presbyterian Catechising* carries the same message. Similar pictures can be found in galleries across Scotland. In the Dundee City Museum there is a delightful canvas by R. McGregor bearing the title *The Story of the Flood*, illustrating the way in which the formal teaching of the church was backed up by informal instruction at the level of the home. The same museum contains exhibits illustrating the life of another Scottish

Evangelical missionary whose remarkable work in West Africa is celebrated in a stained-glass window – the redoubtable Mary Slessor. The Aberdeen Art Gallery displays a huge canvas by Sir Edwin Landseer which suggests why the story of the flood might have special resonance in the Highlands. This large painting shows the pain and dislocation suffered by poor families during a devastating flood in the Highlands. Although it has no particular religious significance it does introduce us to another very power-ful set of images often used to delineate Scottish culture: the land of mountain and flood, of tartan, kilts and heather. Incidentally, there is a connection between this painting and the honouring of British war heroes in London so deplored by Spurgeon: Landseer was the artist responsible for the huge lions which guard the foot of Nelson's column in Trafalgar Square.

Let us make one more stop in our Edinburgh quest for an understanding of Scottish culture. We turn out of Princes Street and walk up to the Usher Hall. It is possible that the evening concert there commences with an overture by Hamish MacCunn entitled 'Land of the Mountain and Flood'. This brilliant music was written by a young man only eighteen years of age and gave expression to the composer's sense of pride in Scotland. In fact the second half of the nineteenth century witnessed a great surge of distinctively Scottish music: Alexander Mackenzie's 'Scottish Rhapsody', John Blackwood McEwen's *Solway* Symphony, the patriotic symphonic poems of William Wallace, and the *Celtic* and *Hebridean* Symphonies of Granville Bantock. In all these works (which are only now beginning to be appreciated after years of neglect) there is an evocation of the glories of rural Scot-land. There is also, especially in Bantock, a typically romantic desire to recover ancient, pre-Christian traditions, to return to what is believed to be the 'Gaelic vision'. One of Bantock's works is called the *Pagan* Symphony.

This brief survey of public art in Edinburgh highlights two of the strands which contribute to the making of Scottish cultural identity. In the first place, the question 'What is Scotland?' can be answered geographically. It is a territory, a place which can be identified on the map of the British Isles and an area whose beauty has been depicted in literature, music, photography and, not least, by the tourist industry. The sense of belonging to a particular place is an important dimension in the creation of cultural identity and one which has nurtured and sustained Scottish national pride while also significantly shaping perceptions of Scotland in the wider world. However, we need to be aware of the possibility that the presentation of Scotland as 'land of mountain and flood' can involve a selective approach to historical realities. The comment of John Prebble on the emptiness of the Highlands is unforgettable: 'In all of Britain only among [the Scottish hills] can one find real solitude and if their history is known there is no satisfaction to be got from the experience.' He goes on to say that 'while the rest of Scotland was permitting the expulsion of its Highland people it was also forming that romantic attachment to kilt and tartan that scarcely compensates for the disappearance of a race to whom such things were once commonplace reality'. These moving words suggest that there is substance in the warning expressed by Neal Ascherson: 'We talk easily about the forging of a nation, but forgery has played a real part in the foundation and revival of many nations.'

The second influence on Scottish culture which is evident from a casual walk down Princes Street relates to the religious tradition stemming from the Reformation. Symbolic reminders of the importance of the Calvinist vision of a godly commonwealth in which the whole life of the nation was to be permeated by biblical values are to be found throughout Scotland. William Storrar observes that the original motto of the city of Glasgow – 'Let Glasgow Flourish By The Preaching of the Word of God and the Praising of His Name' – reflects John Knox's vision of national reformation and encapsulates the unique Scottish religious-cultural ethos. The Edinburgh statues of Chalmers and Guthrie are important reminders of a time when Evangelical Calvinism had a profound impact on the culture, while the public recognition of missionaries like Livingstone and Mary Slessor bears witness to the fact that Scotland provided a base from which a world-transformative Christianity spread around the globe.

The ministries of Chalmers and Guthrie are important in relation to our subject precisely because their work was done during the floodtide of early modernization when the forces unleashed by the Enlightenment and the industrial revolution challenged both the validity and the viability of the social vision of the Scottish Reformation. Chalmers moved from rural Fife to a city experiencing the kind of explosive growth in population which is today reported in the burgeoning urban centres of Africa, South America, and Asia. By the middle of the nineteenth century the population of Glasgow had increased twelvefold since 1775; it was almost to treble again by 1911. Guthrie arrived in Edinburgh from Tayside and discovered a situation which, according to one observer, left every visitor with two impressions: 'a sense of [Edinburgh's] extraordinary beauty and a horror of its unspeakable filth'. Here are the ambiguities of modernization: increasing wealth side by side with grinding poverty, the transformation of the material conditions for human existence, accompanied by the fragmentation of society and the erosion of human dignity and worth. What lessons can we learn from Chalmers and Guthrie as they wrestled with such issues at a time of massive cultural change in Scotland?

Both men were of course outstandingly gifted preachers. Some years back I chanced upon two volumes of Chalmers' *Lectures on the Epistle to the Romans* in a second-hand bookshop and was astonished to discover the freshness and originality of his exposition across a gap of well over a century. Reading sermons like these, one realizes why thoughtful people wrestling with new challenges to faith in an era of rapid and profoundly disturbing intellectual and social change found Chalmers' sermons so helpful. His preaching was magnetic among the urban middle classes. His constant and passionate insistence that the possession of wealth brought huge responsibilities was, in Smout's words, ' an inspiration to generations of soul-searching men to give generously of their money and time'. Guthrie was scarcely less able as a preacher. His powers of oratory were legendary and could stir deep emotions. On one occasion he described a disaster at sea in such vivid terms that a sailor in the congregation leapt up and removed his coat, ready to plunge in to save the drowning.

However, there were significant differences between these men when it came to cultural analysis and the application of the Gospel to socio-economic problems. Chalmers' political conservatism is well known. He absolved what he called 'the wealthier orders of society' from all responsibility for the degradation of the urban poor and defended the social *status quo* on the grounds that, 'The structure of human society admits of no other arrangement.' Speaking to working-class parishioners in Glasgow, Chalmers lavished praise on a social order in which the monarchy was 'borne up by a splendid aristocracy, and a gradation of ranks shelving downwards toward the basement of society'. He was equally uncritical in his advocacy of *laissez faire* economics, committing himself to the extraordinary claim that selfishness 'is the grand principle on which the brotherhood of the human race is made to hang together'. Statements like these led to Chalmers gaining the doubtful distinction of being the only Scottish Evangelical singled out for attack in the writings of Karl Marx.

Dr Guthrie's approach was very different. His remarkable book *The City its Sins and its Sorrows* reveals a deeply compassionate man who is able to think new thoughts and seek fresh solutions. Guthrie's analysis of the social injustices which threatened the cohesion and stability of Scotland is both lucid and passionate. Using modern terminology one could argue that Guthrie recognises both the structural dimensions of evil, and that he writes with a 'bias toward the poor'. He argues, for example, that the destitute classes of Glasgow and Edinburgh are doubly deprived of justice for, on the one hand, they live in conditions of such squalor that they are driven to seek food by any means possible, while on the other hand, respectable society exacts retribution from them for crimes which are traceable to its own heartlessness and indifference: 'we first condemn them to crime, and then condemn them to punishment. And where is the justice of that?' Guthrie asks equally searching questions concerning economics: attacking 'a system of trade which offers up our children in sacrifice to the Moloch of money and builds fortunes in many instances on the ruins of public morality and domestic happiness'.

The contrasting responses of these two great preachers to the problems resulting from the impact of modernization suggests that Evangelical religion can take very different forms. It can buttress the *status quo*, offering a religious justification for things as they are, and so become an ideology, or it can function as a counter-culture, exposing injustice and offering a radically different vision of human society derived from the perspective of the Gospel. As Scottish Christians face the challenges of bearing witness to Christ in a situation of renewed cultural flux brought about by the collapse of modernity, it is well to recall the contrasting aspects of their tradition, symbolised by the two Edinburgh statues.

Dr. Guthrie died in 1873 at a time when traditional Christianity seemed under increasing threat. However, in the twentieth century the Enlightenment tradition has come to be challenged as its grand promise of universal human happiness has proved a mirage. The term 'postmodern' is a recent invention but it now seems obvious that the credibility of the culture of modernity has been eroded over a long period of time. Anyone who doubts this should read Eric Hobsbawm's history of the twentieth century, *Age of Extremes*. This important book is prefaced with a series of quotations in which well-known people assess the twentieth century. The late Isaiah Berlin comments, 'I remember it only as the most terrible century in Western history.' William Golding suggests it has been 'the most violent century in human history', while Yehudi Menuhin observes that the twentieth century 'raised the greatest hopes ever conceived by humanity, and destroyed all illusions and ideals'. The ambiguities and tensions of modernity, already evident in the nineteenth century, have become more and more obvious and painful. Modern man can walk on the moon and explore the depths of the cosmos, but he seems powerless to prevent the evils of genocide in Bosnia or Rwanda, or of infanticide in Liverpool, Dunblane or Belgium. To be modern, writes Marshall Berman, is 'to experience personal and social life as a maelstrom, to find one's world and oneself in perpetual disintegration and renewal, trouble and anguish, ambiguity and contradiction: to be part of a universe in

which all that is solid melts into air'. If at the end of the nineteenth century there were growing numbers of people who found
it difficult to believe in God, the problem now has become how
to continue to believe in man.

How has this general cultural crisis in the Western world
affected Scotland? We should perhaps remember here that the
original motto of the city of Glasgow ('Let Glasgow Flourish By
The Preaching of the Word of God and the Praising of His
Name'), so characteristic of the Reformed vision of a godly society, was truncated to become a materialist slogan – 'Let Glasgow
Flourish'. So far as Edinburgh is concerned, the really powerful
cultural symbols are now located on the opposite side of Princes
Street to Dr Guthrie's statue. In a recent survey of 7000 people in
six countries, 88 per cent identified the corporate symbol of the
McDonald's hamburger chain while only 54 per cent could
explain the significance of the Christian cross. No contemporary
cultural analysis can ignore the forces of global capitalism,
symbolised by the illuminated shopfronts of Marks and Spencer,
Disney, Virgin Records and McDonalds, which increasingly
shape Scottish culture, as they do cultures around the world.

Clearly then, an understanding of Scottish culture informed
solely by the romantic perception of the Highlands or by the
religious traditions of the past is bound to be partial, if not fundamentally misleading. This is an important point for Christians
outside Scotland since one can still find people who express the
belief that 'real' religion is to be found at the Celtic 'peripheries' of
the British Isles. Believers struggling with the consequences of the
erosion of a living and public faith at the metropolitan centre may
seek solace in a romantic notion that pure traditions of Reformed
Christianity, or revivalism, or even Celtic holism, remain intact
and unsullied by modernity in the Highlands. But to depict modern Scotland as the 'Land of Reformers and Covenanters' is to
construct a romantic myth no less misleading than certain
versions of the 'Land of mountain and flood' story.

In order to illustrate this point we return to Scottish art and
music. The Museum of Modern Art in Edinburgh displays Ken
Currie's *Glasgow Triptych: Template of the Future*. The canvas

depicts, according to the artist, the decline of the radical socialist tradition which has been a significant force in modern Scotland. Currie's painting shows an old man slumped in a Glasgow bar, drowning his sorrows in the realization that genuine social transformation will not come about through radical political action. At the centre of the picture a young boy plays with a model of a black aircraft, an ominous symbol of the violence of mechanised warfare soon to engulf and divide Europe. In the same gallery we find Peter Howson's *Just Another Bloody Saturday*, which deals with a rather different form of substitute religion which has had considerable salience in Scotland – professional football. Commenting on the rise of football clubs in nineteenth-century Scotland, T.C. Smout observes that the game seemed to arouse exactly the heart-warming zeal and total devotion which ministers of the Gospel 'had tried so hard, so painfully and so totally unsuccessfully to arouse for God'. Howson's canvas though, with its disturbing portrayal of a baying crowd, depicts terrible anger rather than zeal; whatever enjoyment there may be in this Saturday afternoon escape from everyday reality, it seems as empty and insubstantial as the artificial light streaming from floodlight pylons which are the only sources of illumination in the picture.

So far as the contemporary music scene is concerned, Scotland has produced a number of thoughtful rock bands whose lyrics express the same erosion of hope and the sense of human lostness so movingly depicted on the canvasses in the Museum of Modern Art. In so far as such groups express convictions that are widespread among the present generation, they challenge the romantic myths concerning Scottish culture to which reference has been made earlier. Groups like Del Amitri and The Lost Soul Band express the pain of a generation aware of the hollowness of life in a world where, to quote the former, 'Nothing ever happens, nothing happens at all'. The loss of human dignity and the erosion of a sense of purpose in life may be temporarily suppressed by the activism of the day, but 'We'll all be lonely tonight and lonely tomorrow.' For the Lost Soul Band this desperate sense of emptiness actually precipitates a quest for God:

D'you think God has changed with the times?
Does he understand restless feelings?
Does he understand mine?
Does he know half the world doesn't pray anymore?
Does he know half the people don't quite know what to say anymore?

Many recent works of Scottish fiction bear similar testimony to the
tragedy of life in the godless wastelands of our times. In a fascinat-
ing article on contemporary Scottish literature Beth Dickson has
examined a series of modern novels, comparing them with classical works like Scott's *Old Mortality* and James Hogg's *Justified
Sinner*. Commenting on James Kelman's *The Bus Conductor
Hines*, she notes, 'The only remnants of Christianity in the world
he describes are a few of the names of God repeatedly taken in
vain.' After discussing the work of Kelman and other modern Scottish writers like Alisdair Gray and William McIlvanney, she concludes, 'A working knowledge of Christianity has disappeared.'

What are the implications of this brief survey of contemporary
culture for the mission of the Church in Scotland today? I would
like to identify three issues, framed in the form of questions, that
seem unavoidable in regard to mission in Scotland's changing
society.

First, *what is the future of the pulpit in Scotland given the fact
that in the wider culture communication increasingly employs
visual symbols?* As the Edinburgh statues have shown, the preaching of the Word of God has been absolutely central within the
Scottish religious tradition since the Reformation. At times within
the Reformed tradition the sermon became almost synonymous
with the act of worship itself, the gathering of the congregation for
worship being known as 'the time of the sermon', or 'the time of
prayers and preaching'. A tradition in which the preached Word is
so central faces some difficult questions today: can traditional
preaching survive in an era of multi-channel TV, the global spread
of new information technologies, and a shift in public education
from texts to images, from books to screens?

Before attempting to answer that question we may note that
the problems of preaching in the context of modernity have long

been noted. In 1946 a prisoner of war returning home commented on attending church that it seemed as though a glass cover had been placed over the pulpit. 'This smothers all sound. Around the pulpit our contemporaries are standing. They too talk, and they call. But on the inside this is not understood. The glass cover smothers all sound. Thus we still see each other talk, but we don't understand each other anymore.' The great German preacher Helmut Thielicke wrote at length on the post-war crisis facing the Reformation tradition of preaching. Ministers invariably seemed to perform their public ministry 'almost to the exclusion of any public notice whatsoever'. There was, he said, a 'tremendous contradiction' between the conviction that they are called to proclaim a message that would revolutionize life and, on the other hand, the 'utter immovability of the deeply rutted tracks in which they must move'. Thielicke lamented the chasm that existed between the pulpit and the everyday world of those who still chose to sit beneath it. Sermons so often betrayed the fact that ministerial life seemed to isolate preachers within an archaic culture shaped by Christendom, leaving congregations unable to make any connection between what was heard from the pulpit and the struggles, dilemmas and questions arising from daily life in a secular culture.

Warnings like these suggest that if we wish to answer my question concerning the future of preaching by a ringing affirmation of its non-negotiability as the means of Christian communication, we will still need to look seriously at the style and content of the sermon. However sound the exegesis of Scripture may be, unless there is a dynamic, living contact between the message of the Bible and the world in which men, women and young people actually live and work, then Thielicke's prediction of the death of preaching will be fulfilled.

However, I do not think this response goes far enough. Not for a moment do I wish to deny the place of powerful preaching in the purposes of God; I believe gifted expositors who possess a deep understanding of contemporary realities may still break into modern culture with a message of hope, reconciliation and freedom. At the same time, we dare not ignore the shifts that have taken place in this culture as the result of the massive technological changes in recent times. Many analysts believe that we are living through a cultural transformation at least as significant as that which occurred with the invention of the printing press in the sixteenth century. That invention facilitated a transition from oral and visual forms of communication to a culture shaped by printed texts. Luther seized the opportunities created by this new technology to such an extent that it is impossible to think of the spread of the Reformation apart from Gutenberg's printing press.

My question is simple: why should the church at the close of the twentieth century not employ the new technologies now shaping our culture for the sake of the kingdom of God? Why should the electronic superhighway not become a 'way of the Lord'? It is simply impossible to reply that the Bible sanctions nothing but preaching as the means of Christian communication. The Bible does nothing of the sort; it is far from being limited in this way to a single channel of communication. From Genesis to Revelation we find an infinitely rich variety of communication, including story, dream, proverb, vision, as well as sermon. It is a biblical text that affirms 'Ears that hear and eyes that see – the Lord has made them both' (Prov. 20:12). In an era when, whether we like it or not, our children's lives are being shaped by visual imagery, through TV, film and video, Scottish Christians cannot afford to ignore the implications of this proverb.

My *second* question is this: *what is the future of the church in Scotland, given that the culture is now religiously plural?* As we have seen, for many people in modern Scotland, notwithstanding the spiritual glories of the Reformation and the revivals in the past, even the memory of God has now faded. The vacuum left by the decline of institutional Christianity is filled by a bewildering variety of beliefs, whether these are secular substitutes for religion, or various non-Christian faiths. I have met policemen in Aberdeen who swear by the *I Ching* and had long discussions on a train out of Edinburgh with a teacher who described his personal spiritual quests at Findhorn.

In this changed cultural context, the ideology of Christendom, which sustains the belief that in some sense Scotland remains a Christian nation actually forms a barrier to the fulfilment of the church's missionary calling. The 'glass cover' described earlier has become a distorting mirror, blinding believers to the realities of a deeply secular and pluralist society, while presenting unbelievers with an image of Christianity that is a travesty of the revolutionary community described on the pages of the New Testament. Kierkegaard was surely correct when he said that Christendom removed the offence, the paradox, from the gospel and so transformed Christianity into something entirely different from what it is in the book of the Acts of the Apostles.

Is it not obvious that the longer Christians cling to the fiction of Christendom and allow their approach to witness and evangelism to be shaped by this defunct ideology, the greater the danger that the Christian faith will die away in large parts of Scotland? This point has been made very clearly by William Storrar in his ground-breaking book, *Scottish Identity: A Christian Vision*. He calls the Church of Scotland to abandon its pretensions to be the national church in order to become a confessing, witnessing community. The absence of missionary assumptions in the Reformed view of the church has led to a deep crisis for the kirk because it has 'hung on to a view of its identity which looks increasingly shipwrecked in the secular tides of the late twentieth century'. There must be a fundamental shift from being the Church of Scotland to become the Church for Scotland. The kirk must 're-think its Christian identity as the community of those who confess Jesus as Lord, with a distinctive life from the rest of the secular community and yet with an overriding sense of responsibility for that nation in mission, social criticism and service'.

This prophetic call to mission has a resonance far beyond the Church of Scotland. Other denominational traditions, including those which have formally dissented from the established church, have been influenced by the Christendom model in all kinds of ways. For example, the appeals made in evangelistic services among the Baptists or the Plymouth Brethren invariably assume a knowledge of God and an underlying familiarity with the Gospel story which suggests that the so-called 'free' churches are as distant from social reality as the Church of Scotland. The urgent need therefore is for the whole people of God in Scotland to be renewed in unity, truth and love, to shake off the chains which still bind them to an outmoded and unbiblical conception of the church, and be liberated to engage in authentic, costly service in mission in the context of Scotland's changing culture.

In relation to Christian witness in modern Scotland, it is impossible to avoid some comment on the constitutional issue. I speak here with considerable caution but some observations from an Englishman who has lived two miles south of the border throughout the devolution debates may be helpful. Actually, living beside the border between two nations is an interesting experience. I have often recalled the profound observation of the Russian poet, Yevtushenko: 'I suppose that in the beginning men defined borders and then borders began to define men.' It is a comment that warns us of the great danger of a nationalism that becomes idolatrous. Given the condition of Scottish culture as we have described it, there is a very real possibility that people lacking a transcendent reference point for their lives make the love of nation a new locus of the sacred. Christians on both sides of the border need to be alert to the dangers of a pseudo-religious nationalism which makes demands that no disciple of Christ can possibly concede.

At the same time, it is surely legitimate for men and women to 'define borders'. That is to say, socio-political structures are not absolutes; they belong within the sphere of human culture and are open to discussion, critical analysis and change. In a shifting historical and cultural context, rigid political structures may suppress entirely legitimate human aspirations and, at worst, become oppressive. I fear that the political conservatism of Thomas Chalmers and other Evangelicals at a critical juncture in British social history may have actually accelerated the process by which our culture became secularized. It matters a great deal where Christians come down in the argument when, at crucial points in history, there are opportunities to enact social change which could lead to a more just ordering of society. This being so, it is imperative that Scottish Christians contribute to the ongoing debate concerning Scottish identity. Indeed, I hope that such discussions north of the border may stimulate a long overdue engagement in serious theological reflection in the south on what it means to be English.

My *third* and final question is this: *what is the nature of mission in a culture that is both post-modern and post-Christian?*

Mission in a culture pervaded by nihilistic hopelessness and by increasing levels of violence requires a humble and penitent church prepared to face rejection and suffering. The murder of the Anglican priest Christopher Gray outside his parish church in Liverpool vividly illustrated the point. In a moving tribute entitled 'Sense of Mission', Adrian Hastings quoted an essay published by this young pastor just before he was killed: ministers, he said, need to 'be like Christ in the faithful service of their flocks; even to the point of sacrificing their own lives'. Men and women undertaking the task of Christian leadership today must see this, not as one career option among others, but as the call of Christ to authentic, apostolic ministry involving costly service and real personal risk. If this call to mission is refused, if we remain in captivity to a culture wedded to the worship of Mammon, continuing to delude ourselves and others that this culture is in some sense 'Christian', then the church in Scotland really will face death. Christianity may survive as a privatized religion providing a warm glow to a minority who opt for it, but as a living, world-transformative faith it will be extinguished. The light will have gone out. In this scenario serious social criticism may be left to Muslims, who often perceive all too clearly the entanglement of Christianity with Western materialism and find it impossible to take our God-talk seriously. Sociologists have suggested that we are already well down the path that leads to the death of socially significant religion; they argue that all the evidence shows that whatever value evangelical conversion may have in the lives of individuals, its cultural significance is increasingly marginalized.

However, while the crisis facing Christianity in the West in general, and in Scotland in particular, is all too real, it also presents us with a unique opportunity, a *kairos*. At this critical point we may return to first principles, recovering the gospel and learning afresh what it means to be the disciples of Christ in a hostile environment. Such moments of opportunity do not last long and the issues which require to be faced if we are to rise to challenge of mission in Scotland's changing culture need to be placed at the top of our agendas.

Four

Crying in the Wilderness – Preaching in a Post-Christian Cultural Context

'... it is the assumption of virtually all existing work of evangelism that it takes place 'within Christendom' ... Across the stream, we suspect a bridgehead of a friendly power in the dialogue-partner, and we think that we can consolidate and expand through *appeal* and *memory* – an appeal to what still lies dormant ... We will have to abandon all these precious presuppositions ... There is nothing left that can be called into memory, nothing that can be awakened. What still might be present as a residue is usually only some sort of forced image of a caricature Christendom. With that one has become immune to the real thing.'

J.C. Hoekendijk

In this chapter I want to explore some of the dilemmas and challenges facing preachers in the context of our contemporary culture. Nearly thirty years ago the great German theologian preacher Helmut Thielicke published a book with the title *The Trouble with the Church: A Call for Renewal*. The first chapter bore the heading 'The Plight of Preaching' and opened with these words:

Anybody who keeps in mind the goals which the Reformation once set itself can only be appalled at what has happened in the church of Luther and Calvin to the very thing which its fathers regarded as the source and spring of Christian faith and life, namely, preaching.

Thielicke's analysis of the problems facing preachers has lost none of its power and relevance over the years. We have already noticed his description of pastors as haunted by the feeling that their ministries are performed 'to the exclusion of any public notice whatsoever'. Thielicke mentions the reaction of a fellow theologian who bemoaned the absence of academics from other faculties from the Sunday worship of the church before adding, 'But when the sermon is over, I usually say to myself: What a good thing that none of them was there!' Doubtless Thielicke would agree with a more recent writer who, having examined modern preaching from the perspective of communications science, makes the pungent observation that 'the sermon hangs on, shorter perhaps, but oblivious to the difference it doesn't make'.

The question to be considered here then concerns the causes of the crisis facing the pulpit: what are the factors peculiar to the modern world, which make the 'ministry of the word' so difficult today?

Preaching in a changed cultural context

At the end of the 1960s Francis Schaeffer warned Evangelicals that they would need to do 'a great deal of heart-searching as to how we may speak what is eternal into the changing historical situation'. Massive shifts within Western culture had left the churches stranded as sub-cultural minorities alienated from a generation shaped by a consistently secular worldview. 'In crucial areas', Schaeffer said, 'many Christian parents, ministers and teachers are as out of touch with many of the children of the church, and the majority of those outside, as though they were speaking a foreign language.' Unfortunately, these words fell largely on deaf ears, especially among Christians most deeply committed to the 'ministry of the word'. Yet in the intervening years the cleavage Schaeffer had detected between historic Christianity and contemporary Western culture has widened into a chasm with the result that his prophetic call to mission can no longer be ignored. Clearly, the context within which the word of God must be spoken today is different from those in which Calvin, Spurgeon, or even Lloyd-Jones, did so. The question is: How has it come about that churches have been left stranded as subcultural islands and preaching has ceased to be recognised as a form of public discourse, but is rather confined to the shrinking circle of those who 'speak the language'?

At the beginning of this century the classical sociologists Max Weber and Emile Durkheim attempted to analyse the revolutionary changes which were occurring in modern, industrialized societies. Both men recognized that the cultural shifts taking place in the modern world raised questions of critical importance for the future of humankind. Weber's work is especially valuable with regard to our discussion. He believed that the growth of rational thought and the emergence of the 'bureaucratic mentality' were leading to the 'disenchantment' of the world. That is to say, traditional religious beliefs and ideas were being forced into a wholesale retreat before the advancing forces of scientific explanation and rational organization. However, instead of hailing this as a sign of progress (as an earlier generation had done) Weber was deeply aware of the ambivalence of the advance of modernity. The erosion of religious beliefs and their cultural marginalization raised questions of the most serious nature with regard to the future of human societies. Indeed, in a famous phrase Weber predicted that developments in modern culture would result in people eventually finding themselves locked into an 'iron cage' of rationality which would threaten all meaningful human existence. Christians concerned about the plight of preaching at the close of the twentieth century can hardly fail to be moved when listening to this great sociologist wondering whether, at some point in the future, 'entirely new prophets will arise' to herald a 'great rebirth of old ideas and ideals'. On balance Weber is inclined to a much more pessimistic prognosis, anticipating a descent into what he calls 'mechanised petrification, embellished with a sort of convulsive self-importance'.

At the close of the twentieth century we are bound to conclude, alas, that no new prophets have arisen, nor have 'old ideas' revived. Weber's reference to prophecy is particularly painful for evangelical preachers because it focuses our attention on precisely the area of greatest weakness in modern preaching. Weber once described himself as 'religiously tone deaf' yet he clearly knew the biblical tradition well enough to be fully aware of the significance of the term 'prophet'. It is both moving and disturbing to find this great thinker wondering whether it might be possible that, in the barrenness of a one-dimensional culture, someone might stand up and utter words possessing the power to break open the secular worldview and expose it to another, transcendent reality. Almost a century later we must ask: where are the preachers who speak with such prophetic authority? To be sure, many have claimed that prophetic gifts have been restored to the church, yet the content of such 'prophecies' prove on examination to be at best trivial, at worst contemporary parallels to the notorious preachers known to the Old Testament who merely use the name of the Lord to buttress the *status quo* and leave a secular culture completely undisturbed.

The failure of modern preaching to address contemporary rellity is all the more tragic given the depth of the moral and spiritual crisis of the Western world. The Oxford sociologist Bryan Wilson, working within the Weberian tradition, has analysed contemporary culture with undisguised anxiety and pessimism. Modern people, he writes, have been learning 'how to live without a culture, or with the rags and tatters of an earlier culture still clutched about the parts of us that we least care to expose'. Wilson suggests that an integrated culture may have become a thing of the past and he concludes: 'We know no moral order to give meaning to our social order. We have lost faith in the vision of a cumulative and progressive culture which cherished the products of the human spirit, elevated man's humanity, guarded the inheritance of past societies, and rejoiced in the widening prospect of the richer inheritance of posterity.'

Here are recurring themes of modern intellectual debate: the collapse of a shared sense of conviction concerning the purpose of human life, the absence of any agreed foundation for morality, and the erosion of hope resulting in a sense of the absurdity and tragedy of human existence. Moreover, the analyses of the sociologists are paralleled by the yet more anguished depictions of modern life on the part of writers, artists and musicians. We shall discuss this in more detail in the following chapter, but the note of despair in modern culture can be detected in many of the greatest novels of this century, it can be heard in the music of composers like Gustav Mahler and is reflected in the bleak canvasses of any number of modern artists. Perhaps nowhere is this desperate loneliness more movingly portrayed than in the work of the American painter Edward Hopper. His *Nighthawks* is a terrifying picture of the lostness of people in the industrialized, urban wilderness. Moreover, as we advance into the new millennium, what was once a nightmare anticipated by writers and artists possessing peculiar insight has become the common experience of men and women, and especially young people, at all levels of society. Lesslie Newbigin describes the fulfilment of Weber's prophetic vision, the iron cage within which we celebrate the arrival of a millennium in the absence of a story that gives that event meaning: 'There is overwhelming evidence of a loss of faith in any worthwhile future, a loss of any sense of meaning, of any sense of the sacred.'

Earlier in this century as it became evident that the churches were losing their grip on the British population, the residual influence of the Sunday School movement provided a shared context of ideas, making possible the assumption that the masses absent from worship at least knew their Bibles and understood the Gospel story. Thus, provided outsiders could somehow be coaxed back into the churches, there was no fundamental problem of communication. However, as the Dutch theologian J.C. Hoekendijk indicates in the quotation at the head of this chapter, there is nothing left that can be called into memory, nothing that can be awakened. Welsh rugby crowds no longer know how to sing hymns, the pre-match ritual of the singing of 'Abide with me' at Wembley has finally been recognised as a cultural relic from an era now long past, and even in the leafy suburbs of the south-east of England (or in the Celtic fringes of the Scottish Highlands) the realities of secularization have become inescapable.

Preaching to the converted

In the cultural situation we have described, one great temptation facing preachers is to turn inwards, to direct ministry solely to the task of the nurture of the 'little flock'. Preaching can too easily become a purely internal affair, employing the language and idioms understood within the church and making minimal contact with the wider culture. This tendency is increased when the work of ministers isolates them from the realities of a secular world within which the members of their congregations must live day by day. When not in the pulpit, many conscientious pastors are to be found in the study preparing to preach, or in the homes of their flock engaged in pastoral visitation. Contacts outside this restricted circle will include fraternals of ministers where one meets with those who are 'like-minded'. All of this is doubtless worthy and desirable, but ministerial isolation from the concrete realities of life in contemporary society inevitably results in a type of introspective preaching which leaves even the most faithful members of the congregation struggling to discover connecting links between what is heard from the pulpit on Sunday and the demands of life in the world throughout the week. Listening to sermons one often wonders whether preachers have the slightest idea of the ethical dilemmas facing the businessmen in their audience, or whether they appreciate the intellectual doubts which may be troubling teachers or students who have encountered modern critics of theism, or how far they are aware of the massive pressures which the youth culture creates for the teenage sons and daughters of their members.

I suggest therefore that it is crucial that preparation for preaching in the context of the modern world must involve not only a concern with correct exegesis and exposition of the text of Scripture, but an appreciation of the peculiar challenges and temptations with which modern culture confronts Christians. Pastors must not only speak to the people in their congregations, they must also listen to them. Thielicke said of himself that as a preacher he was engaged in 'an unending dialogue' with those to whom he was called to deliver the message. Such a dialogue may occur informally as part of the normal interaction between a pastor and his people, or it may be built into the structure of church life, thus providing a formal feedback mechanism by means of which communication through preaching may become effective, relevant and powerful.

Of course, the problem discussed here raises serious questions concerning the training of preachers. Those who have responsibility for the preparation of people called to a ministry of preaching at the close of the twentieth century must ensure that their students know both the Word and the context in which it is to be preached. This underlines the point made earlier concerning the nature of theological education today. While the importance of specialized training for men and women called to minister in cross-cultural mission among people of other faiths in exotic locations has always been recognised, there is now an urgent need for ministries which equip churches for mission in the post-Christian culture of the Western world. There is also a need for the re-training of preachers whose ministries have been shaped by patterns of study which provided them with valuable exegetical skills without ever enabling them to deal with apologetic or missiological questions, or introducing them to the basic principles of effective cross-cultural communication. The ecclesiastical debris of a ruined Christendom which, like a containing dam, prevents the waters of life from irrigating the deserts of modernity, must be cleared away and the preaching of the Word must be related in powerful and imaginative ways to the concrete realities of a fragmented, pluralist and post-Christian culture.

There is a further insight from the discipline of sociology which can assist us in understanding the pressures faced by preachers today. Since the European Enlightenment the dominant intellectual tradition in the West has excluded God and the supernatural from what is generally accepted as 'knowledge'.

Deism placed God at the outer edge of the cosmos, a 'First
Cause' retained in order to plug the remaining gaps in scientific
knowledge and explanation. From here it was a short step to a
totally empty and silent universe and Nietzsche's declaration of
the 'death of God'. Religious truths which had once operated at
the heart of European culture now became marginal; indeed,
they were no longer accorded the status of 'truths' at all, becoming instead merely the private beliefs of people who found them
comforting and reassuring. Meanwhile, quite different 'truths'
moved into the public realm; politics, law, economics, education,
all now began operating apart from absolute moral principles
and without regard to the biblical message proclaimed by
preachers.

It is precisely at this point that Christians face a painful
dilemma; if preaching retains the concepts and language of the
pre-modern era it risks complete marginalization, but if it begins
to seek relevance by adaptation to the ruling ideas of a secular
world, it is headed toward extinction. The American sociologist
of religion, Peter Berger, describes the first of these options as fol-
lows: 'If one is to go on proclaiming the old objectivities in a social
milieu that refuses to accept them, one must maintain or construct
some sort of subsociety within which there can be a viable plausi-
bility structure for the traditional affirmations. What is more, the
subsociety must be carefully and continually protected against
the pluralistic turbulence outside its gates. Put a little rudely, one
must maintain a ghetto.' We are reminded of Thielicke's observation that pastors find themselves exercising their ministries
'almost to the exclusion of any public notice whatever'. The crucial question here is whether it is possible, in the specific context
of a pluralist culture, to construct an effective apologetic for faith
which does not involve capitulation to secularism? The history of
the church in the West in the twentieth century surely demon-
strates that 'accommodation' of the classic liberal kind is a path
that leads theology into an abyss; it is literally suicidal. At the
same time, the kind of conservatism which leaves the Gospel
locked firmly within a ghetto cannot be an option for those who
take Christ's summons to mission seriously. To continue using

the language and idioms of the nineteenth century (or, even worse, the sixteenth century) when preaching in the context of our nihilistic age involves an abdication of Christian responsibility to communicate the Word of Life to those who most need to hear it. As Thielicke observes, those who are content to transmit 'the conventional and familiar, unchanged and undigested' are actually guilty of laziness and unfaithfulness. Laziness, because the labour of interpretation and translation is hard work and it is 'never done without abortive trials and breath-taking risks'; unfaithfulness, because merely to repeat old phrases is in fact to give people stones instead of bread. Thankfully, Evangelical theologians have begun to engage in what Mark Noll calls 'a patient effort to think through major questions of Christian belief in relation to significant theories and compelling practical needs of the modern world'. Preachers must utilise such theological reflection and strive to apply the eternal word to the realities, dilemmas and spiritual longings of our postmodern age.

Preaching and the renewal of the church

In the 1950s and 60s Britain witnessed unprecedented prosperity and it seemed that never-ending economic expansion was one of the givens of life in modern society. This was the context for what has come to be called the 'expressive revolution' – a concerted attack on limits, conventions, roles, form, structure and ritual. It was, says Bernice Martin, 'the pursuit of ambiguity and the incarnation of uncertainty'. Young people declared their freedom from the restrictions of traditional thought and morality; the boundaries between 'right' and 'wrong' became fluid, and appropriate behaviour was now determined by the 'feel-good' factor rather than by any external ethical codes. Indeed, subjective feelings became enormously important; words like 'experience' and 'atmosphere' cropped up again and again (BBC radio sports commentators frequently invite us to 'listen to the atmosphere'!). Ideas which had been in circulation among an intellectual élite since the beginning of the twentieth century now began to permeate popular culture.

Inevitably these changes began to be reflected in various ways in the churches. David Bebbington has pointed out that many aspects of the charismatic movement are symptomatic of a cultural ethos that 'stressed immediacy (and) the human capacity for instant heightened awareness'. By shifting the centre of gravity in contemporary Christianity away from objective truth and toward subjective experience, the charismatic movement mirrored trends within society as a whole and can be described as a religious expression of cultural modernism.

The cultural shifts of the 1960s thus sparked widespread reconsideration of inherited patterns of life and worship within all the churches. At the close of the decade Francis Schaeffer published *The Church at the End of the Twentieth Century* – in which he warned Christians that they must stop debating the issues of yesterday and prepare for 'the real changes that lie ahead'. Many writers urged the development of patterns of congregational fellowship which would facilitate the growth of Christian community and highlighted the shallowness and inadequacy of the *koinonia* in traditional congregations. There were demands for radical reform in the structures of church life, in forms of worship and calls for the rejection of inherited concepts of ministry. In *New Wineskins: Changing the Man-made Structures of the Church*, Howard Snyder asked, 'What if there is something basically wrong with the traditional concept of ministry in the church?' Like many others at this time he concluded that received patterns of ministry which required pastors to act like spiritual superstars were indeed fundamentally flawed and unbiblical. Ministers too often created bottlenecks, preventing the development and exercise of a whole range of spiritual gifts within the congregation. 'It is time' Snyder said, 'to go back to the Word to find a biblical ecclesiology, a biblical concept of the church compatible with the new stirrings of the Spirit in our day.'

In some circles the call for the renewal of the churches led to a form of subjectivism which resulted in overt hostility to preaching and even a devaluing of the authority of the written Word itself.

These trends clearly mirrored the direction taken by the coun-ter-cultural movement in the wider society – the rejection of forms and structures, the priority of feeling and emotion over thought and will, and a diminished interest in objective truth. The danger of an uncritical adoption of modernist culture was brilliantly described by Os Guinness in his *The Gravedigger File*. The Christian faith, he says, is in great danger of losing its intrinsic value and becoming almost purely instrumental in purpose: it is prized for what it does rather than for what it is. Sadly, the form and content of much contemporary worship, the appeal to self-interest in a good deal of modern evangelism and the perva-sive subjectivism and hedonism in Christian literature indicates that sectors of the Evangelical movement are shaped by the values of consumer society. Not surprisingly, such an environment is uncongenial to biblical preaching.

However, if the 'Body-Life' emphasis has been distorted in the manner just outlined, a retreat to the traditional *status quo* can-not be the correct response. The fundamental re-evaluation of the doctrine of the church, of the nature of ministry, and of patterns of worship to which reference has been made has provided a wel-come opportunity to recover lost and neglected biblical insights. The challenges presented by a changing culture do have to be faced if churches are not to be locked into patterns of life and practice which result in their dismissal as the cultural relics of a bygone era. As cross-cultural missionaries know well, questions arising from the encounter between the Gospel and cultures very often open our eyes to aspects of the biblical record which had previously been overlooked or ignored. It would be surprising if the challenge of mission in the context of modern culture did not lead to reform as we discover neglected aspects of the apostolic model of the church.

In this respect we can surely be thankful that certain inherited notions of 'ministry' have been challenged. It has been said that for too long the church has resembled a sporting event in which twenty thousand people desperately in need of exercise come to watch twenty-two men desperately in need of rest! Pastors have sometimes understood their role in a manner which has prevented the development and exercise of a rich variety of congregational gifts. Patterns of worship involving the recognition of varieties of gifts may bring pressures on preaching, but they are also capable of liberating pastors to fulfil their true function in teaching the word of God. To be set free from the need to pretend that one is omnicompetent is both a relief and a step toward a more truly biblical pattern of ministry. The utilisation of congregational gifts in worship, in specialised ministries among children and youth, in counselling, in a range of caring activities, and in endless other ways, enables preachers to focus on their calling to minister 'the word and doctrine'. It will also mean that more time can be spent interacting with a world that is in such desperate need of the truth; thus the ministry of the Word may begin to address the real issues of contemporary life in a manner that could lead to a genuine revival of biblical preaching.

Preaching and communication

In the previous chapter I suggested that perhaps the biggest challenge facing preaching today arises from the technological revolution through which we are now living. Can preaching retain credibility when technological, social and cultural changes are occuring which appear to leave monologue teaching isolated as a relic from the past? Is the pulpit not as archaic as the wooden school desk with its inkwell, now found only in museums?

Before we jump too quickly to a negative conclusion it is well to consider the response of one of the most brilliant of Christian thinkers in this century, the French philosopher-theologian, Jacques Ellul. Like Max Weber, he was deeply sceptical about claims concerning human 'progress' and, far from accepting that modern man had somehow 'come of age', Ellul repeatedly warned that the end-product of our much-vaunted scientific and technological progress would in fact be dehumanisation. Few other Christian thinkers in modern times have matched Ellul for the profound depths of his analysis or the prophetic manner in which he has spoken to the church. In his view, the unceasing expansion of technology into every area of our lives reduces words to mere 'utilitarian ciphers' and creates a pop-culture in which meaning is replaced by rhythm. As mathematical thought takes priority over all other forms of reasoning, Ellul prophesies that the growing dominance of the computer will complete the work of 'mental destruction' which has been in process throughout the twentieth century. In this context, he summons Christians to recognise and overcome the temptation to capitulate to a technological culture by creating communities of resistance, nurtured by 'the humiliated word'. Christians in the Third World have come to similar conclusions and, in an ironic reversal of the situation in which they were on the receiving end of missionary exhortations to avoid illicit syncretism, they now warn us of the threat posed to the Gospel by a technological culture. Thus, René Padilla, while recognizing that technology has a legitimate place in mission, says that problems arise when 'technology is made a substitute for Scripture under the assumption that what we need is a better strategy, not a more biblical Gospel and a more faithful church'.

Clearly, these warnings must be heeded. Nonetheless, a legitimate concern to preserve the centrality of the word of the Lord should not lead us to ignore the real challenges which must be faced by those who wish to communicate with modern people. Again, there are helpful insights to be drawn from the experience of cross-cultural missions. Among tribal peoples Christianity has often been criticised as 'too cerebral' a religion and as a faith which restricts its blessings to the literate. The charge has some substance in the light of the practice of Protestant missions. Yet Scripture itself testifies to the employment of a rich variety in the forms of revelation: prose and poetry, sermon and song, symbol and parable – all these and more are employed to convey the word of God. Certainly the Bible is concerned to inform the mind and move the will, but it also operates at the level of the human imagination and appeals to the affections. The book of Revelation, for example, has been described as the most important piece of social-cultural resistance literature in the ancient world, yet it achieves its purpose by purging and renewing the imaginative life of the early Christians. Confronted at every turn by the symbols of Roman power and tempted to capitulate to the myths of an empire that prided itself on being the goal of human history, the early churches found in the Apocalypse an alternative symbolic universe which enabled them, like John on the Isle of Patmos, to reject Roman definitions of reality and to live in the light of a very different story. We do not compromise or downgrade preaching by recognising the crucial importance of the imaginative dimension in Christian communication. In fact, although the Protestant tradition has tended to discourage the recognition and use of people with such gifts, it might be argued that those who have been able to employ dreams, stories and myths to convey God's eternal word have had an impact both on the church and in the wider culture rarely matched by either academic theologians or traditional preachers. John Bunyan and C.S. Lewis are examples that immediately spring to mind.

It is thus important that we recognise that the written word, like the incarnate Word, is wonderfully adaptable and reflects the grace of the God who, in Calvin's phrase, 'prattles with us in an awkward and common style'. The Bible provides us with clear precedents for effective communication to pre-literate societies and, in so doing, offers principles and models that will enable us to face the challenge of making the word of God known to people who increasingly appear to belong within the category of the post-literate.

Preaching and the preacher

It is impossible to deal with contemporary pressures in ministry without, finally, considering the dangers confronting the preacher as an individual. Cases of ministerial burn-out or of serious moral failure are now so common as to absolutely demand that we give attention to the pressures on the preacher. In an age like ours pastors are likely to face acute problems, whether the obvious moral dangers peculiar to those who find themselves placed in positions of trust, to intellectual doubts which, for very obvious reasons, a pastor may attempt to suppress, or the constant danger of slipping into a routine which conceals an ever-increasing spiritual dryness at the core of one's own being.

The psychologist Erich Fromm describes the way in which emotionally disordered people frequently become dangerously dependent upon a professional person seeking to help them, regarding a doctor or therapist as someone with 'magic' powers. Fromm's description of this process has obvious application to pastors:

> The relationship looks like love; it is often accompanied by sexual desires; yet it is essentially a relationship to the personified magic helper, a role which obviously a psychoanalyst, like certain other persons who have authority (physicians, ministers, teachers), is able to play satisfactorily for the person who is seeking the personified magic helper.

At a time of cultural crisis and moral chaos, when ministers are liable to find themselves dealing often with the casualties of a secular society, these words should give us pause for reflection. Preachers, by virtue of the public nature of their work, may easily become the focus of such disordered longing and expectation and they require great wisdom and caution when, in the privacy of study or vestry, they counsel people who are inclined to invest such hopes in them. This is a contemporary pressure on the ministry of the Word we dare not overlook. It also compels the question (especially urgent in relation to traditions of ecclesiastical Independency), 'Who pastors the pastor?'

At the conclusion of this chapter I want to return to the diagnosis of contemporary preaching provided by Helmut Thielicke. With rare brilliance he analyses the intellectual, theological and communicational failings of the modern pulpit. However, he concludes that when all is said and done, the distrust of Christian preaching is ultimately to be located in the fact that 'the man who bores others must also be boring himself'. Thus, Thielicke says, the trouble with modern preaching 'lies deep in our actual spiritual condition, in a pathological condition of our spiritual existence'. As long as we have not conquered this 'sickness unto death', which is seated in our unconvincing Christian existence and nowhere else, then 'all secondary remedies are meaningless and restricted to very innocuous symptom-therapy'.

Five

Voices from the Wilderness

'We stand on the shore of an ocean, crying to the night and the emptiness. Sometimes a voice answers out of the darkness, but it is the voice of one drowning, and in a moment the silence returns. The world seems to me quite dreadful.'

Bertrand Russell

As we have seen, the culture of the West at the close of the second millennium is fragmented to such an extent that some analysts question whether it merits the description 'culture' at all. Not surprisingly in this situation, there is no consensus among Western thinkers about human nature; indeed, contemporary theories concerning humankind propose diametrically opposed views. In the absence of God man has become a problem. Where the psalmist could ask in wonder and amazement, 'What is man that you are mindful of him?', modern people living in a culture that has declared God to be dead, simply ask in confusion, 'What is man?'

The basic dilemma: man between heaven and earth

Christians have always recognised that human beings are defined and distinguished by two fundamental characteristics. On the one hand, they are creatures – they belong within creation and are subject to the limitations of nature and of death. At the same time, humans possess self-consciousness and, uniquely among created beings, are aware of the transcendent. In the words of Koheleth in Ecclesiastes, despite radically secular worldviews and hedonist lifestyles men discover an ineradicable sense of eternity set within their hearts.

However, where Christianity held these two dimensions together in creative tension, secular anthropologies swing wildly between one and the other. At one extreme we find a naturalistic reductionism which focuses on man as a biological organism in such a manner as to explain human nature away. At the other end of the scale there is a romantic self-deification which ignores the earthiness of man and encourages him to indulge in dangerous fantasies. The post-Christian world cannot make up its mind about the human person, says Stephen Evans. It cannot decide whether the human person is a monster to be tamed or a god-like creature who must simply be freed to express or 'realize' its own innate potentialities.

This secular dilemma has been expressed with great clarity by Ernest Becker. In his remarkable book *The Denial of Death*, he shows how Renaissance thinkers stressed the divine-like qualities of man, emphasising those characteristics which clearly separate human beings from nature. But, Becker says, this same being is also 'a worm and food for worms'. Man is a terrible paradox, 'out of nature and hopelessly in it . . . up in the stars and yet housed in a heart-pumping, breath-gasping body'. Excluding both God and eternity from view, secular thought struggles to come to terms with this paradox. As Becker puts it, 'Man is literally split in two; he has the awareness of his own splendid uniqueness in that he sticks out of nature with a towering majesty, and yet he goes back into the ground a few feet in order blindly and dumbly to rot and disappear forever.'

Becker claims that the basic driving force in modern culture is man's fear of death. An illustration of this can be seen in the tragic words of Simone de Beauvoir: 'I think with sadness of all the books I've read, all the places I've seen, all the knowledge I've amassed and that will be no more. All the music, all the paintings, all the culture, so many places: and suddenly nothing . . .' However, before we consider those who, like de Beauvoir, have openly faced the reality of death, we need to note an influential theory of man which suppresses this feeling of terror.

Man as machine

The view I wish to note here has been described as 'scientific humanism'. In sharp contrast to the ethical humanism which strives to retain the dignity and freedom of man, this theory emphasises biological conditioning and denies the traditional claim that human beings are unique. According to scientific humanists, man is embedded within nature, locked into the evolutionary process. Everything previously understood to be distinctive and unique in humankind is explicable in terms of genetic conditioning. B.F. Skinner, the distinguished American psychologist, deliberately distanced himself from classical humanism by giving his most famous book the provocative title, *Beyond Freedom and Dignity*. Skinner argued that modern anthropology was trapped between an outmoded traditional philosophy of human nature and a consistently scientific view of man. Discredited notions of human freedom and responsibility must be replaced by a consistent materialism in order that rational, scientific social planning and management may come into their own.

As the prestige of science has been eroded in recent years, such deterministic theories of human nature have lost favour. However, views similar to those of Skinner continue to be advocated, notably within the discipline of socio-biology. Richard Dawkins, for example, argues that science is perfectly capable of dealing with all the classical questions concerning the meaning and purpose of human existence. He quotes with approval a zoologist who claimed that all attempts to answer questions like 'What is man?' or 'What are we for?' prior to 1859 should be completely ignored. Dawkins' view of the human person is thus clearly based on evolutionary biology and leads him to conclude that 'we, like all other animals, are machines created by our genes'.

The moral and ethical implications of such a theory become plain when Dawkins writes, with disarming honesty, that the 'universal love and welfare of the species as a whole are concepts which simply do not make evolutionary sense'. Furthermore, if there is no such thing as human nature, if people possess no dignity which distinguishes them from other species, then my death is, quite literally, no different from that of a dog. Clearly, the way is open here for genetic engineering and for the attempt to create a utopian society by means of what Skinner called 'behavioural technology'. So far as the beginning of life is concerned, Dawkins states that the notion that the human foetus can claim some special protection over that accorded to an adult chimpanzee 'has no proper basis in evolutionary biology'.

It is difficult to judge the extent of the influence of scientific humanism of this kind. On the one hand, such a reductionist view of man runs counter to the mood of our times according to which people are encouraged to break free from the limits of nature by means of a plethora of quests for the transcendent. On the other hand, the impact of such ideas should not be underestimated; in areas like penal theory, medical research and the treatment of mental disorders, behaviourist ideas often underlie practices which involve treating people like machines.

'Ye shall be as gods'

If one stream of secular thought flows toward the pole of 'nature' and defines the human in terms of rootedness within the world, the other moves toward the opposite pole and proclaims the divinity of man. Nietzsche, whose philosophy has been extremely influential among artists and writers, explicitly denied that man is the result of special design or purpose. In his view, the 'death of God' demanded the emergence of a new race of men who would take upon themselves the task of recreating the world. Nietzsche wrote, 'Once you said "God" when you gazed upon distant seas; but now I have taught you to say "superman".' Karl Marx also saw God as an obstacle to the liberation of man and understood his socio-political project in explicitly Promethean terms. 'Religion', said Marx, 'is only the illusory sun which revolves round man as long as he does not revolve round himself.' These nineteenth-century thinkers really did believe that man could and should replace God and that, in doing so, the way would be opened to a new world of freedom, justice and happiness.

It did not take long however for the realization to dawn that modern man, alone in an empty cosmos, now carried a crushing burden of responsibility. Nietzsche might exult in the task facing the human race in the absence of God, but for those who followed him, the profoundly negative consequences of man's attempt to rule the world soon became plain. We have already seen how Max Weber, anticipating the stifling growth of bureaucracy and rationality, was overcome by pessimism with regard to the human condition. Jean-Paul Sartre, in a famous phrase, described modern people as 'condemned to freedom'. Albert Camus, one of the most honest and courageous of all modern writers, saw the tragedy of post-Christian man in terms of the ancient myth of Sispyhus. Having stolen the secrets of the gods and put death in chains, Sisyphus was condemned endlessly to push a rock up a hill, only to watch it repeatedly roll back again. So, Camus said, modern man has paid a terrible price for his freedom; like Sisyphus 'his passion for life won him that unspeakable penalty in which the whole being is exerted towards accomplishing nothing'. This note of nihilistic despair can be heard in the music of composers as different as Vaughan Williams and Shostakovich and is reflected in the bleak canvasses of European artists like Picasso and Edvard Munch.

However, in addition to bearing the burden of despair and loneliness which is the lot of secular man, contemporary thinkers must also explain why the liberation from ancient restraints and superstitions proclaimed by Nietzsche and Marx actually opened the floodgates to barbarity and violence on a scale unprecedented in history. How is it, to be precise, that man was no sooner pronounced free from the obligation to worship God, than he allowed a succession of human tyrants to place new chains around his ankles? Why was it that, at the very point at which people aspired to become like God, Europe fell under the control of fascism, Nazism and Stalinism? The psychologist Eric Fromm addressed this issue in his book *The Fear of Freedom* and concluded that while the culture of the West provided individuals with certain external liberties, it actually left them more isolated, anxious and powerless than ever. 'Behind a front of satisfaction and optimism', Fromm wrote, 'modern man is deeply unhappy; as a matter of fact, he is on the verge of desperation.' People so terrified of the freedom offered to them in the modern era become easy prey for 'hero' figures whose ideologies provide a sense of meaning and purpose and whose charisma and power give security to the anxious. Eric Fromm offers an enlightening diagnosis of our times and reminds us of the fragile nature of our civilization and the continuing vulnerability of modern man to the claims of false messiahs.

The hedonistic alternative

As Koheleth realised long ago, faced with the stark terrors of life in a godless universe most people will turn tail and take flight from reality, immersing themselves in activities which provide a shield against the truth of existence. In this connection it has to be said that if we wish to understand the modern wilderness we will need to spend time reading the tabloid press as well as studying the kind of works cited above. Actually, little has changed from the time of Ecclesiastes; money, sex and drugs still provide the escape routes for people who lack the strength to look death in the face. Pascal, who observed the restlessness of modern people with such insight and sympathy, wrote, 'Being unable to cure death, wretchedness and ignorance, men have decided, in order to be happy, not to think about such things.' What is new today is the range of technologies by means of which the 'silence of eternity' can be shattered and rational thought and reflection rendered impossible. The lack of quietness, the sheer volume of noise now taken for granted in the West, whether piped into shopping malls or emanating from a million Walkmans, is itself testimony to the futility of life 'beneath the sun'. Ernest Becker neatly sums up the modern flight from reality when he says, 'Modern man is drinking or drugging himself out of awareness, or he spends his time shopping, which is the same thing.'

'A being reaching out beyond himself'

As the Enlightenment project to build a new world of freedom and happiness on a humanist basis has foundered, psychologists and sociologists have asked whether this failure may indicate that modern, Western culture overlooked something fundamental in human nature. Peter Berger, for example, argues that secularized worldviews appear to frustrate deeply grounded human needs, including 'the aspiration to exist in a meaningful and ultimately hopeful cosmos'. In similar vein, Becker observes that the every-day food quest alone cannot still human restlessness: 'The cycle of eat, fight, procreate, and sleep – that absorbs the members of other species – has only the barest meaning for man.' Albert Camus developed his 'philosophy of the absurd' on the basis of two fundamental convictions – that it is impossible at present to discern any meaning in the world, and the painful recognition that the human heart continues to ache with longing for just such a transcendent purpose. Camus' atheism is very different from that of Nietzsche and leads him to say, 'The certainty of a God giving meaning to life far surpasses in attractiveness the ability to behave badly with impunity. The choice would not be hard to make. But there is no choice and that is where the bitterness comes in.' The significant point here is that Camus' anthropology recognizes both man's deep longing for a meaning that transcends this life, and the extreme difficulty of living in the world without such knowledge.

Another important witness to the human need to discover a meaning to life which transcends present experience is the psychotherapist Viktor Frankl. The fundamental problem facing many of his patients, Frankl concluded, was not physical or psychological by nature, but 'spiritual'; people were unable to face life because they had no way of making sense of it. Frankl

described 'existential frustration' as 'the collective neurosis' of
our time, a profound crisis at the level of meaning which was
incapacitating modern people and leaving them in a state of
dis-ease and boredom. At the same time, Frankl observed that
despite their frantic search for pleasure, people remained unsatisfied and bored and it was evident to him that happiness forever
eludes those who make it the object of their lives. Happiness,
Frankl insists, is a by-product of the discovery of the ultimate
meaning of my existence; when made into the goal of life it
becomes an idol which will turn to dust in my hands. Thus,
Frankl concludes that the quest for ultimate meaning is a definitive mark of the human person: 'The essentially self-transcendent
quality of human existence renders man a being reaching out
beyond himself.'

The challenge of preaching in the modern wilderness

In view of the crisis facing modern people in the context of a culture which is manifestly unable to satisfy the human craving for
meaning, what response should theology and Christian preaching
make?

First, I suggest that there is need for a sympathetic understanding of the dilemmas confronting modern people.
Unfortunately, theology in general, and evangelical theology in
particular, still wears the clothes and speaks the language of the
ghetto. It remains largely an internal business divorced from the
apologetic and missionary task which should, in an age such as
this, be its primary concern. Our ears must be open to the cries of
pain and despair coming from contemporary writers and artists.
Take, for example, this description of grief on the part of one of
John Fowles' characters on hearing the news that his girlfriend
has died: 'Staring out to sea, I finally forced myself to stop
thinking of her as someone still somewhere . . . but as a shovelful
of ashes already scattered, as a broken link, a biological dead
end, an eternal withdrawal from reality, a once complex object
that now dwindled, dwindled, left nothing behind except a

smudge like a fallen speck of soot on a blank sheet of paper . . . I did not cry for her . . . but I sat in the silence of that night, that infinite hostility to man, to permanence, to love, remembering her, remembering her.' Given such a tragic view of humankind, preaching must be characterised by compassion, cultural relevance and a servant-like determination to engage in serious dialogue with a generation which knows itself to be facing the abyss.

Secondly, I suggest that we need to be cautious in speaking about God. I am not proposing that Christian preaching should become defensive or inhibited in its witness to faith, far from it. And yet, there is a shallow triumphalism which, for all its apparent certainty, is desperately lacking in reality. The late Klaus Bockmuehl, responding seriously to the Marxist critique of religion, said 'we must show that God is not just a language event . . . When we speak of the reality of God, we tend to sound as though we are talking about life on Mars – no one knows much about it and even if one did, it would not make a difference in everyday life.' Jacques Ellul, who has a way of putting his finger on the right spot, wrote a book entitled *Hope in Time of Abandonment* in which he said that, reviewing the work of the churches over the past century, he had the feeling of being in front of a very bad orchestra! Ellul insisted that in the present crisis, Christians needed to feel the tragedy of the withdrawness of God from Western culture: '. . . what I see is that we are abandoned by God. Oh I do not say forever, or that we are excluded from salvation, but that here and now in this moment of history, in this night which perhaps has refused the light, no actual light is shining any longer.' If Ellul is correct, then preachers must not only seek relevance, but they must spend time on their knees with the cry of the psalms of lament on their lips – asking God 'Why?' and 'How long?'

Thirdly, given the absence of consensus in our culture concerning the nature of the human person, the doctrine of humankind is clearly of critical importance. However, we cannot simply repeat the formulations of the past since, as is well known, it is precisely Christian teaching concerning the uniqueness of humankind which has come under sustained critical scrutiny in recent years. We must listen to our critics and not dismiss out of hand the charge that, by stressing man's separateness from other species and his right to rule creation, historical Christianity must take some responsibility for the looming ecological catastrophe. We should acknowledge that certain approaches to anthropology in the history of theology, based on a distorted understanding of the concept of the 'image of God', have played a part in creating a technological society in which, as Douglas John Hall says, it is almost impossible to 'live like the truly human beings exemplified by the One who walked with his disciples in the wheat fields and slept in a storm-tossed boat and ate fish from unpolluted waters'. The fact is that Scripture provides a secure basis for an understanding of personhood which, rather than threatening the earth, stimulates responsible stewardship and grateful respect. More than that, when the *imago Dei* is understood biblically, so that man regains his sanity only as he enters into a relationship of love and obedience with his creator, then Christian theology has in its hands a message with the potential to renew hope and bring new life to a despairing age. In words that are surely remarkable coming from a humanist, Ernest Becker wrote at the conclusion of his last book: 'If we were not fear-stricken animals who repressed awareness of ourselves and our world, then we would live in peace and be unafraid of death, trusting to our creator God and celebrating his creation.' It is our privilege to tell modern people that just such a life of freedom and hope is possible as we recognise our status as forgiven sinners and sons and daughters of the Father.

Six

Finding a Way Through the Wilderness: Evangelical Christianity at the Close of the Twentieth Century

'The new in history always comes when people least believe in it. But, certainly, it comes only in the moment when the old becomes visible *as* old and tragic and dying, and when no way out is seen. We live in such a moment; such a moment is *our* situation.'

Paul Tillich

At the beginning of this century the writer Arnold Bennett published a novel with the title *Anna of the Five Towns*. The story concerns a young woman who seeks, without success, to experience religious conversion in the context of traditional Methodist revivalism. Bennett describes how, in a desperate search for a personal experience of God, Anna attends evangelistic meetings only to find that the preacher's appeals leave her cold and unsatisfied. In a passage which probably reflects his own alienation from the Evangelical religion of his parents, Bennett depicts Anna trying to imagine what it might be like to be converted, or to be in the process of being converted:

> She could not. She could only sit, moveless, dull, and abject . . . In what did conversion consist? Was it to say the words 'I Believe'? She repeated to herself softly 'I believe, I believe'. But nothing happened. Of course she believed. She had never doubted or dreamed of doubting, that Jesus died on the cross to save her soul, her soul, from eternal

damnation . . . What then was lacking? What was belief? What was faith?

Bennett's novel was published in 1902 and it contained an implicit warning that traditional Evangelicalism was losing contact with a changing culture. However, this warning went largely unnoticed and unheeded; chapels were still well-filled and although a few children of believers might, like Anna, go the way of the world, it remained possible to suppose that well-tried methods of evangelism were adequate to ensure a continuing harvest of converts. Indeed, by the end of the first decade of this century the delegates to the great missionary conference held in Edinburgh in 1910 could speak with confidence of 'the evangelization of the world in this generation'.

From our vantage point at the close of the century it now seems clear that the sensitive antenna of an artist like Arnold Bennett correctly detected the condition of the British churches even before the cataclysm of 1914–18 changed the world forever. The problem for the churches today is no longer how to respond to a relatively minor slippage in relation to the children of the chapels; the chapels themselves have gone, or are in the process of going. The stark reality of the situation facing institutional Christianity at the present time is expressed in the haunting words of a recent poem by the Welsh writer R.S. Thomas. The poem is entitled 'The Chapel':

> A little aside from the main road,
> becalmed in a last-century greyness,
> there is the chapel, ugly, without the appeal
> to the tourist to stop his car
> and visit it. The traffic goes by,
> and the river goes by, and quick shadows
> of clouds, too, and the chapel settles
> a little deeper into the grass.
>
> But here once on an evening like this,
> in the darkness that was about
> his hearers, a preacher caught fire

and burned steadily before them
with a strange light, so that they saw
the splendour of the barren mountains
about them and sang their amens
fiercely, narrow but saved
in a way that men are not now.

Thomas' striking image of the chapel, once ablaze with revival fires but now settling 'a little deeper into the grass' corresponds to the analyses of a growing number of theologians and sociologists who warn that the crisis now facing institutional Christianity in the Western world is one of truly massive proportions. Here is David Mills, an American Episcopalian, who uses almost apocalyptic language to describe the plight of Anglicanism: not only has the fat lady sung, 'but the cleaners have left, the security guards have turned out the lights and locked the doors, and the wrecking ball waits outside for tomorrow's demolition work. But even so, a few men and women in purple shirts . . . still huddle together in the now dark stalls, chatting excitedly of all the great operas they are going to stage.' This prediction of ecclesiastical meltdown is endorsed by the New Zealander Michael Riddell in a recent book: 'The Christian church is dying in the West.' Believers, reacting as bereaved people often do to a great loss, may deny this reality, bolstered by 'small outbreaks of life', yet it is beyond doubt, says Riddell, that institutional Christianity in the Western world is afflicted by a terminal sickness.

These comments refer, you will notice, to denominational Christianity. My concern in this chapter however is with Evangelicalism, the cross-denominational tradition which emerged from the great revivals of the eighteenth century, stressing personal conversion, belief in the truthfulness of the Bible, and a life of active service to God and neighbours as the core elements of authentic Christianity. It might be argued that this tradition, newly enlivened by the fires of charismatic renewal, forms an exception to the negative assessment of modern religion to which reference has been made. It might be possible, for example, to cite evidence of the phenomenal success of the Alpha Course, or the surge in new churches in many parts of Britain, or the growth of the Spring Harvest events, or the steady rise in 'born-again' religion in the United States as indications that Evangelicalism is immune from trends toward decline and secularization afflicting more traditional denominational religion.

I view such claims with considerable scepticism. The late Klaas Bockmuehl observed that Christians in general had given little serious thought to the challenges posed by secularization and he noted that Evangelicals were often content 'if they add to their numbers even when the overall state of Christianity deteriorates'. In fact, the born-again phenomenon in America suggests that it is possible for very considerable numbers of people to profess conversion without such a movement resulting in any significant change in the surrounding culture. In the words of David Wells:

> The vast growth in evangelically minded people in the 1960s, 1970s, and 1980s should by now have revolutionised American culture. With a third of American adults now claiming to have experienced spiritual rebirth, a powerful countercurrent of morality growing out of an . . . alternative worldview should have been unleashed in factories, offices and board rooms, in the media, universities, and professions . . . But as it turns out, all this swelling of evangelical ranks has passed unnoticed in the culture . . . the presence of evangelicals in American culture has barely caused a ripple.

The reason for this of course is to be found in the fact that American Evangelicalism no longer appears to possess an 'alternative worldview' to that which operates at the heart of the culture. At the beginning of the 1960s the sociologist Peter Berger noted that American churches had become prosperous because they provided religious support and sanction for the secular values which dominate everyday life and work in society. In a striking passage Berger observed that a child growing up in a suburban, church-going family in modern America bears 'an uncanny resemblance to the young Buddha whose parents shielded him from any sight involving human suffering or death'. In such a situation the prophets or poets who point to 'the darkness surrounding our clean little toy villages' are regarded as 'candidates for psychotherapy'.

The question which inevitably arises here concerns the definition of the term 'evangelical'. Has this word been gutted of its original meaning? Has it become a mere slogan, divorced from the truths and values derived from the gospel of Jesus Christ? Is it the case, as David Wells claims, that Evangelicals are among those who are on the easiest of terms with the modern world and so have lost their capacity for dissent? Questions like these are being asked not only in North America but on this side of the Atlantic as groups like the 'Reform' movement in the Church of England and the recently founded coalition operating under the banner 'Essentially Evangelical' sound increasingly strident alarms. Today a question that would previously have been unthinkable is being asked in all seriousness: is the Evangelical tradition coming to an end? After two hundred years during which it has demonstrated its ability to challenge and renew cultures, as well as bring hope and healing into the lives of millions of people, has this particular historical manifestation of the Christian faith become a spent force, restricted to a cultic role and powerless to challenge a dominant culture which is in the grip of hideous idolatries? Is Evangelicalism facing a junction, or a terminus?

The end of the line?

In attempting a response to these crucial questions I want to make use of a number of different perspectives. First of all, from a *sociological* point of view it must be admitted that the prognosis does not seem to be encouraging. As we have seen, sociologists have noticed that it is possible for a movement like Evangelicalism to experience significant numerical growth without this affecting the dominant values and ethos of a secularized culture in the slightest way. Thousands of people may claim to be born-again, yet business goes on as usual. Jesus may be praised as Lord in lively and joyful celebrations on Sunday, but the counter-cultural values of the kingdom he proclaimed seem to be non-transferable when it comes to the realms of education, the media, advertising, business and commercial activity. The technical term used in sociology to describe this change in the function of religion is privatization. According to Bryan Wilson, modern religious revivals 'have no real consequence for other social institutions, for political power structures, for technological constraints and controls. They add nothing to any prospective reintegration of society, and contribute nothing towards the culture by which a society might live.'

This may seem to be a harsh and negative judgement, yet it compels us to ask whether a resurgent Evangelicalism is capable of transforming and renewing modern culture? Is there any evidence that this movement, fragmented by the empire-building of its constituent parts and weakened by a persistent strain of anti-intellectualism, might be capable of challenging the fundamental values of a deeply secular society? Is it conceivable that Evangelicalism might resist and destroy the monstrous idols which extend their control into every aspect of our economic and social life? And can we really believe that it might discover the spiritual, moral and intellectual strength needed to be capable of offering the world at the dawn of the third millennium a radically new and hopeful vision of human existence, shaped by beliefs and values that would lay the foundation for a culture characterized by love, compassion, justice and life lived within limits? It would a bold person, I suggest, who answered these questions affirmatively. On present evidence we might as easily anticipate that Evangelicalism will move toward a greater syncretism with Western culture, abandoning the possibility of ever again being a force able to transform the world for the glory of God.

The second perspective from which to attempt to answer our question concerns the *cultural* factor. Given the commitment to worldwide mission that has marked the Evangelical movement from its inception, issues surrounding the relationship between the gospel and cultures have been of constant interest and concern. As we saw in chapter one, two hundred years ago William Carey and his colleagues were determined to ensure that churches resulting from their cross-cultural transmission of the Christian faith should take a recognizably Indian form. Their insistence that the gospel must be contexualized, that Indian believers should be encouraged to express both the content and the form of their faith in ways that were Asian, led to tension between the missionaries and their supporters in Britain. Very few Evangelicals today would deny the wisdom and validity of Carey's approach to mission and it is generally recognised that churches should be 'deeply rooted in Christ and closely related to their culture'.

However, while assent may easily be obtained for this principle when it relates to churches in other cultures overseas, the issue becomes problematic and painful when we ask the question: To which culture do our churches relate? Or to put it another way, can Evangelicalism meet the challenge of a valid contextualization of the gospel for Western culture at a point at which that culture is passing through dramatic and far-reaching change? Paraphrasing the apostle Paul, someone recently described the struggle to comprehend contemporary culture as one in which 'We see through a kaleidoscope darkly.' Western culture at the close of the twentieth century leaves us 'bewildered by shifting patterns of family and household living, short-term and part-time unemployment, multi-channel television and multi-screen entertainment, the global media and information highways . . . seven-day shopping in cathedral-like shopping malls . . . alternative therapies and new age spiritualities, the rainbow of single issue campaigning groups and a myriad of other cultural trends'. In this situation, says William Storrar, writing about the challenges facing the Church of Scotland, 'the local parish Kirk can seem as anachronistic as the traditional High Street grocer's shop, the Edwardian music hall or the nationalised coal mine, a relic of another age'.

In this connection, I think of the church in which I grew up and was nourished in the Christian faith. The building in which we worshipped was erected in the 1880s and was called the Baptist Tabernacle, although anything less like a tabernacle would be difficult to imagine. It was certainly not intended to be portable, a movable sanctuary for a pilgrim people. On the contrary, those who built this enduring Tabernacle were not moving anywhere;

they had just arrived as respected and valued members of bour-
geois society. Today this listed building is overshadowed by a
massive shopping mall and as consumers pour into the Harlequin
Centre every Sunday it is just possible that they may glance at this
striking example of our national religious heritage. This building,
like so many others, erected in an earlier time to the glory of God,
has become a huge obstacle to mission in a postmodern world.
Stranded on the edge of a vast car park serving the consumerist
temple which dominates the skyline, the Tabernacle ironically
appears to symbolise the immobility of the church and its captivity
to cultural forms perceived as outmoded and irrelevant.

I suggest that the challenge which this cultural context presents
to the Christian mission is one of the greatest and most dangerous
ever to have faced the church. On the one hand, it should be possible for a movement which possesses two centuries of accumulated
experience and expertise in cross-cultural missionary endeavour
to discover faithful and creative ways of ensuring that Christ
becomes a living option for a generation shaped by postmodern
culture. This is the concern of people like Dave Tomlinson and
John Drane who argue that Evangelicalism has been so directed
toward the culture of modernity that 'it is being left behind by the
pace of change, and is finding it increasingly difficult to be taken
seriously by the new emerging mainstream Western culture'. On
the other hand, while a fearful retreat to the ghetto is not an
option for faithful Christians, no-one should underestimate the
daunting nature of the missionary challenge presented by
the Western world today. Frankly, I worry about Christians who
treat postmodern culture on very easy terms as though it were a
neutral context likely to prove immediately hospitable to the message of Christ. On the contrary, the West increasingly takes on the
appearance of a vast cultural swamp which threatens those who
wander into it without regard to its dangers with suffocation and
death. The Christian mission has never been a merely human
enterprise and those who have struggled to bring Christ into the
heart of another culture know well the pain and the perils of this
task. Those Christians who rightly take the need to relate the
gospel to the changing culture of the modern West seriously must

also pay attention to the history of mission if they are to avoid the perils of being sucked into the bog of a materialist and relativistic worldview. Perhaps it must also be said that, assuming a re-evangelization of Europe is possible, this cannot be achieved by an evangelistic quick-fix employing new technologies; rather it is likely to be a work of generations, perhaps even centuries.

My third perspective on our question is a *historical* one. Surveying the history of the Christian movement Andrew Walls observes that it reveals that churches can wane as well as rise: 'Areas where Paul and Peter and John saw mighty encouragement are now Christian deserts. The Christian heartlands of one age can disappear within another.' The church in Jerusalem provided the first launching pad for cross-cultural mission, yet it was very soon eclipsed by a new centre of dynamic spiritual life and, retreating to a monocultural expression of the faith, it rapidly became marginal to the purposes of the Holy Spirit. Or consider the case of North Africa: a region which was once home to some of the most significant theologians in the history of Christianity is today identified as being at the centre of the so-called 10/40 window, the least evangelized part of the globe.

Thus, history warns us that no particular local tradition of Christianity is guaranteed survival. An Evangelicalism which loses contact with the dynamic power of the gospel and becomes blind to its own captivity within a secular culture may well be terminally sick. In fact the perplexity experienced by many European Christians today is related to the struggle to recognise that the latest centres of Christian life and growth are located in the non-Western world. Long established habits of thought and practice based on the assumption that the churches of the West occupy centre stage in the purposes of God must be abandoned in the light of this new reality. We now find ourselves standing in the wings, witnessing others take the lead in God's still unfolding drama of redemption. As we have seen earlier, Christians in the Southern hemisphere are well aware of this change and often enquire whether we really understand its significance.

My final perspective may be described as *biblical and theological*. It would not be an exaggeration to say that a fundamental concern of the great prophets of Israel was to challenge the complacency and pride which resulted from a distorted understanding of divine election and to warn their people that they, no less than the surrounding nations, would experience God's judgement if they continued to violate the conditions of the covenant. Consider, for example, Isaiah, who drops a bombshell in Jerusalem at the very start of his prophecy. He addresses the self-confident citizens of a place they regarded as holy and indestructible, 'You people of Gomorrah' (1:10) and declares that God could not bear their 'evil assemblies' (1:13) since they concealed godless lives and hard hearts beneath a cloak of religious respectability. Much later, when the judgement had fallen, Ezekiel has to confront the insane optimism of people who still live with the illusion that the troubles are temporary and will soon be over. To the exiles who refuse to accept reality and try to comfort each other with the assurance that everything will quickly return to normal, Ezekiel is sent to declare one of the shortest and most dramatic texts of the Bible: 'The end has come! The end has come!' (7:7).

The same kind of language is found on the lips of Jesus. Standing in the prophetic tradition he cuts through the façade of religious pretence and warns his hearers that neither centuries of tradition, nor strict adherence to the external duties of religion can provide protection against the Living God who demands of those who profess to know him, love and obedience. Nor are such warnings confined to the religious establishment; Jesus tells his most intimate circle of followers that whenever a religious tradition becomes lifeless and powerless, then however hallowed and loved it might be, the end is near: '. . . if the salt loses its saltiness . . . It is no longer good for anything, except to be thrown out and trampled by men' (Mt. 5:13). At the end of the New Testament, on this side of Calvary and Pentecost, the glorified Christ utters the same warnings to Christian congregations beginning to settle down in the world and making their peace with the dominant culture of the Roman empire. The church at Ephesus, for example, brought to birth a generation earlier in what we might call the fires of revival, is called to repentance and told that it faces a terminus: 'If you do not repent, I will come and remove your lampstand from its place' (Rev. 2:5).

There is one passage in the New Testament which, it seems to me, has a very particular significance in relation to our concerns. In the letter to the Romans Paul wrestles with the mystery of the purposes of God in human history and, in particular, with the problem of the relationship between fallen Israel and the Gentile church. The language used suggests that Paul is aware, even at this early stage in Christian history, that the age-old tendencies toward religious pride and an unlovely arrogance toward other people were surfacing among non-Jewish Christians. In a text which has received less attention than should have been the case and which has an obvious relevance to our question regarding the future of Evangelicalism, Paul says to the Gentile church: 'Do not be arrogant, but be afraid . . . Consider the kindness and sternness of God: sternness to those who fell, but kindness to you, provided that you continue in his kindness' (Rom. 11:17–24).

All change here!

Where then does this analysis leave us? Are we at a junction or a terminus? Is Christianity in the Western world in general, and the Evangelical tradition in particular, beyond hope, beyond genuine renewal? Viewed from one angle the crisis we face seems to be of such proportions that none of the remedies offered in the past promise a solution. Michael Riddell, speaking about New Zealand, says, 'I have lost count of the number of revivalist movements which have swept through my homeland promising a massive influx to the church in their wake. A year after they have faded, the plight of the Christian community seems largely unchanged, apart from a few more who have grown cynical through the abuse of their goodwill, energy and money.'

However, the Christian faith bears a message of hope and the God worshipped through Jesus Christ is amazingly patient, kind and gracious. Jonah had a second chance to respond to this missionary God by recognizing the radically new thing Yahweh was about to do beyond the narrow confines of the elect; Peter had three opportunities to withdraw his protest note against the disturbance caused to his religious world by the missionary priorities of the risen Christ. Moreover, the biblical texts mentioned earlier suggest that in the mercy of God endings are followed by new beginnings. Beyond the agonies of loss and exile Israel hears the word of God which says, 'Forget the former things . . . See, I am doing a new thing' (Isa. 43:18–19). At the point at which the people of God finally accepted that there was no way back to things as they had been, they were able to receive the divine revelation of something radically new. Is this perhaps the kind of situation in which we find ourselves today? The long era of Western Christendom is over and we live amid the remnants of that period, trying to make sense of our situation and confused and disoriented by the complexity of the changes occuring both in society and in the church. Yet even as we despair at what has been lost and grieve over the fragmented and weakened condition of the churches, can we begin to catch the indications that God is inviting us to participate in something quite new?

In September 1996 a conference was held at the University of Aberdeen with the title *The Future of the Kirk*. The conference was reminded that since 1956 the Church of Scotland had lost over half-a-million members, a massive exodus described by one of the speakers as 'the Silent Disruption' of the national kirk. William Storrar analysed this situation and concluded that 'the postmodern Kirk must find in the Gospel its own critique of the postmodern condition in church and society'. Christians are called, he said, to be slaves of Jesus Christ and not slaves of the age in which God has called us to live: 'I am hopeful that a very different Church of Scotland can find new institutional life and purpose . . . and a new evangelical voice and vocation in postmodern Scotland'.

Similar voices are to be heard within the Church of England. In numerous books and articles Robert Warren has called for the building of missionary congregations which move beyond the sterile models of the church inherited from the era of Christendom. If it is to survive in a postmodern society, says Warren, the church must replace a preoccupation with the pastoral care of those who are committed to it with a new focus on participation in God's mission in the world. Once released from the burden of vainly attempting to sustain outmoded ecclesiastical structures, the people of God can develop new ways of being the church which will enable them to fulfil the biblical calling to be what Warren calls 'a pilot project for the age to come'.

Finally, Robert Dunlop, an Irish Baptist pastor who has worked for many years in County Kildare, has called for an end to the cultural captivity of Protestantism in Ireland as a precondition for the discovery of a new way of being the church in a deeply divided society. Writing before the advent of the current peace process, Dunlop observed, 'With the collapse of the institutional-ised church model . . . we are beginning to see the possibilities of the impact of a powerless church which is no longer concerned with exerting authority but in the style of John the Baptist points beyond itself to the King and His Kingdom.'

These voices represent a growing body of opinion across all denominational boundaries that the present crisis offers an unprecedented opportunity to rediscover the true nature of the Christian church and to return to first principles. Might we go even a stage further and suggest that with the collapse of what was regarded as 'Christian civilization' we may also be able to recover what it actually means to be Christian? Jacques Ellul once said that 'Christendom astutely abolished Christianity by making us all Christians' and he went on to claim that in such a culture 'there is not the slightest idea what Christianity is'. The concern to dis-tinguish between 'real' Christianity and its counterfeits in various types of culture-religion has been a central feature of the Evangeli-cal movement. This would suggest that if we do indeed stand at the edge of a situation in which Western Christianity can recover an apostolic vision of the calling of the people of God in this world, Evangelicalism has a crucial part to play in the future. However, in the light of its own compromises with a secular cul-ture it may need to be reconverted, purged of its addiction to the comfortable and undemanding religion which has too often been allowed to replace the demands of discipleship, and renewed through a fresh and wholehearted confession of Jesus as Lord and a determination to live in the light of the values of the kingdom of God revealed in his life, death and resurrection.

What this new situation might mean in detail is impossible to say, except that the church which emerges from this process is likely to have rediscovered its identity as a pilgrim people, living as aliens in a hostile world and (if 1 Peter is to be believed) learning how to 'participate in the sufferings of Christ' (1 Pet. 4:12–13). I dare not pretend to a prophetic knowledge of just how such a development might fit with the redemptive purposes of God, but the possibilities are wonderfully exciting and we, or perhaps our grandchildren, may live to see a renewal of real Christianity in the Western world. I suggest then that it is too early to conclude that Western Christianity, or Evangelicalism, have reached a terminus; rather we stand at a junction and, provided we board the right train, we may commence a journey to a destination never before visited or even imagined.

Seven

Bibliographical Essay

Every effort has been made to identify here the sources of quotations made within the main text of this book. I trust that the information supplied below will prove helpful to readers wishing to pursue this subject further. I have added some suggestions for additional reading although this is obviously far from exhaustive in a field in which the literature is now increasing continually.

Chapter One

The reference in the Introduction to the late Alan Flavelle relates to his article 'The Church – Today and Tomorrow' in the *Journal of the Irish Christian Study Centre* 2 (1984) 27–37. The quotation from Andrew Walls at the head of Chapter One is taken from his *The Missionary Movement in Modern History* (Edinburgh: Edinburgh University Press, 1996). The relevant chapter is entitled 'The Old Age of the Missionary Movement' and is (like much else in this book) a seminal piece of writing. William Carey's *Enquiry* was originally published in 1792; the Baptist Missionary Society produced an edition in 1991 with a facsimile cover and a preface by the missionary historian Brian Stanley (Didcot: BMS, 1991). The quotations from Baptist missionaries in India are from the *Periodical Accounts*, a series of volumes containing the correspondence which passed between Andrew Fuller in England and Carey and his colleagues in Asia. The first volume appeared in 1795. Other primary sources used in writing this chapter were *Brief Narrative of the Baptist Mission in India* (London: E.W. Morris, 1813); William Ward, *Farewell Letters* (London: 1821); and *Missionary Sermons – 1812–1924* (London: Carey Kingsgate Press, n.d.). The extreme form of Calvinism from which Carey escaped is well described by Peter Toon in his *Hyper-Calvinism* (London: The Olive Tree, 1967) and the work which triggered the emergence of a new, evangelical Calvinism was Andrew Fuller's *The Gospel Worthy of All Acceptation*, published in 1786 and reprinted in the 1960s (Ann Arbor: Sovereign Grace Publishers, 1961). The quotations from the American theologian Jonathan Edwards are from *The Works of Jonathan Edwards* (London: Westley and Davis, 1834). Iain Murray's description of the eschatology of the early Evangelicals in his *The Puritan Hope* (London: Banner of Truth, 1971) remains valuable and challenging, while David Bebbington has given us a definitive history of this movement in *Evangelicalism in Modern Britain: A History from the 1730s to the 1980s* (London: Unwin Hyman, 1989).

Chapter Two

The quotation from David Bosch is from his *Believing in the Future: Toward a Missiology of Western Culture* (Leominster: Gracewing Publishers, 1995). I have also drawn on his great work *Transforming Mission* (New York: Orbis Books, 1991). John Mbiti's vigorous call for the liberation of African theology is in his 'Christianity and Culture in Africa' in the volume *Facing the New Challenges* (Kisumu, Kenya: Evangel Publishing, 1978) while the quotation from Choan-Seng Song is in his *The Compassionate God* (London: SCM Press, 1982). The missiological works to which I refer in this chapter include Eugene Nida, *Message and Mission* (South Pasadena: William Carey Library, 1972); David Hesselgrave, *Communicating Christ Cross-Culturally* (Grand Rapids: Zondervan, 1978); Charles Kraft, *Christianity in Culture* (New York: Orbis Books, 1979) and Harvie Conn, *Eternal Word and Changing Worlds* (Grand Rapids: Zondervan, 1984). The quotation from Stanley Hauerwas and William Willimon is from their well-known and widely read *Resident Aliens* (Nashville: Abingdon Press, 1989) and the stimulating discussion of Jeremiah in relation to the devastation of Japan in the Second World War can be found in Kosuke Koyama's *Mount Fuji and Mount Sinai* (London: SCM Press, 1984).

Chapter Three

The quotation heading this chapter is from Douglas John Hall's stimulating study, *The End of Christendom and the Future of Christianity* (Leominster: Gracewing Publishers, 1997). This book, like that from Bosch quoted at the beginning of the previous chapter, belongs in a series edited by Wilbert Shenk under the title 'Christian Mission and Modern Culture'. Every volume published so far in this series suggests that it will come to be seen as a really significant contribution to contemporary theological and missiological debate but, in addition to those mentioned above, I have found the following exceptionally helpful: Alan Roxburgh, *The Missionary Congregation, Leadership and Liminality* (Harrisburg: Trinity Press International, 1997); Gordon Scoville, *Into the Vacuum: Being the Church in an Age of Barbarism* (Harrisburg: Trinity Press International, 1998); Kenneth Cragg, *The Secular Experience of God* (Harrisburg/Leominster: Trinity Press International/Gracewing Publishers, 1998); and Judith Gundry-Volf and Miroslav Volf, *A Spacious Heart: Essays on Identity and Belonging* (Harrisburg/Leominster: Trinity Press International/Gracewing, 1997).

My sources for the discussion of Scottish culture were John Prebble, *The Highland Clearances* (Harmondsworth: Penguin, 1969); William Storrar, *Scottish Identity: A Christian Vision* (Edinburgh: The Handsel Press, 1990); T.C. Smout, *A Century of the Scottish People: 1830–1950* (London: Fontana Press, 1987); Graham Walker and Tom Gallagher (eds.), *Sermons and Battle Hymns: Protestant Popular Culture in Modern Scotland* (Edinburgh: Edinburgh University Press, 1990), and David McCrone,

Understanding Scotland: The Sociology of a Stateless Nation
(London: Routledge, 1992). I also benefitted from Steve Bruce's
No Pope of Rome: Militant Protestantism in Modern Scotland
(Edinburgh: Mainstream, 1985) and his article 'A Failure of the
Imagination: Ethnicity and Nationalism in Modern Scotland' in
Scotia 1992/XVII. The quotations from Beth Dickson and
Donald Meek can be found in articles in the *Scottish Bulletin of
Evangelical Theology*, Spring 1996, 14/1. Thomas Chalmers'
social theology is outlined in his *The Application of Christianity
to the Commercial and Ordinary Affairs of Life* (Glasgow:
Chalmers and Collins, 1820) while Thomas Guthrie's approach
to urban mission is to be found in his challenging and moving
book, *The City – Its Sins and Its Sorrows* (Edinburgh: Adam and
Charles Black, 1857). Eric Hobsbawm's *Age of Extremes* (London: Abacus, 1995) is a masterly survey of the troubled twentieth
century while Marshall Berman describes the ills of modernity
with rare insight in *All That is Solid Melts Into Air* (London:
Verso Press, 1982). My quotation from Jacques Ellul is from his
The Subversion of Christianity (Grand Rapids: Eerdmans, 1986)
and I also referred to Antonie Wessels' two stimulating studies:
Europe: Was it ever really Christian? (London: SCM Press, 1994)
and *Secularized Europe: Who will Carry off its Soul?* (Geneva:
WCC Publications, 1996).

Chapter Four

The quotation with which the chapter begins is from J.C.
Hoekendijk, *The Church Inside Out* (London: SCM Press, 1964).
This volume and Helmut Thielicke's *The Trouble with the
Church: A Call for Renewal* (London: Hodder & Stoughton,
1965) are immensely valuable sources. The same can also be said
for two Evangelical contributions to the debate on the future of
the church and its ministry, Francis Schaeffer's *The Church at the
End of the Twentieth Century* (London: The Norfolk Press,
1970) and Howard Snyder's *New Wineskins: Changing the
Man-made Structures of the Church* (London: Marshall Morgan

and Scott, 1975). Snyder followed up this book with two further studies: *The Radical Wesley and Patterns for Church Renewal* (Downers Grove: IVP, 1980) and *Kingdom Lifestyle: Calling the Church to Live under God's Reign* (Basingstoke: Marshall Pickering, 1986).

The sociological perspectives mentioned in this chapter are provided by Emile Durkheim, *The Elementary Forms of Religious Life* (London: Allen and Unwin, 1915); Max Weber, *The Protestant Ethic and the Spirit of Capitalism* (London: Unwin, 1985); Bryan Wilson, *Contemporary Transformations of Religion* (Oxford: Clarendon Press, 1976); and two works from an American sociologist of religion who knows how to write well, Peter Berger. See his *The Noise of Solemn Assemblies* (Garden City, NY: Doubleday, 1961) and *The Heretical Imperative* (Garden City, NY: Anchor/Doubleday, 1979). I also drew upon Bernice Martin's valuable study, *A Sociology of Contemporary Cultural Change* (Oxford: Blackwell, 1981) and her article 'The Sacralization of Disorder: Symbolism in Rock Music' in *Sociological Analysis*, 1979: 40/2, 87–124. The quotation from Eric Fromm in this chapter comes from his *The Fear of Freedom* (London: Ark Paperbacks, 1984); I have also found much to challenge and stimulate (as well as to provoke) Christian thought in his *To Have or To Be?* (London: Abacus, 1979).

On the music of Gustav Mahler, see David Holbrook, *Gustav Mahler and the Courage to Be* (London: Vision Press, 1975) and the life and art of Edward Hopper (including of course *Nighthawks*) is brilliantly described by Ivo Kranzfelder in *Edward Hopper: Vision of Reality* (Borders Press, 1998).

Os Guinness makes brilliant use of the sociology of religion to analyse the current malaise within Evangelicalism in *The Gravedigger File* (Downers Grove: IVP, 1983), while the first signs of a theological renewal which might enable this tradition to engage contemporary thought in a fruitful way are glimpsed in a book edited by Mark Noll and David Wells, *Christian Faith and Practice in the Modern World* (Grand Rapids: Eerdmans, 1988). Jaques Ellul's distinctive perspective, and his profound critique of technology, can be found in various books including *Perspectives*

/

on Our Age (New York: The Seabury Press, 1981) and *What I Believe* (Grand Rapids/London: W.B. Eerdmans/Marshall Morgan & Scott, 1989). In my view his most brilliant contribution remains *The New Demons* (London: Mowbray, 1975). René Padilla's criticism of Evangelicals' over-dependence on technology was made at the Lausanne Congress and is printed in the volume containing the papers delivered there, *Let the Earth Hear his Voice*, J.D. Douglas (ed.) (Minneapolis: Worldwide Publications, 1975). Padilla later articulated his own theology of mission in *Mission Between The Times: Essays on the Kingdom* (Grand Rapids: Eerdmans, 1985).

Chapter Five

The quotation from Bertrand Russell is borrowed from a lecture given by D. Martyn Lloyd Jones, *Will Hospital Replace Church?* (London: Christian Medical Fellowship, 1969). Unfortunately, I have been unable to trace the original source of Russell's deeply personal statement regarding the hopelessness of a fully secular worldview. Stephen Evans' essay 'Healing Old Wounds and Recovering Old Insights' is contained in the volume edited by Noll and Wells mentioned above. Hans Kung's *Does God Exist?* (London: Collins, 1980) provides an excellent overview of modern thought and deals with most of the secular critics of religion mentioned in this chapter (my quotation of Simone de Beauvoir is taken from this book). My quotes from Richard Dawkins are from *The Selfish Gene* (St Albans: Granada Publishing, 1978); Nietzsche's words are taken from *A Nietzsche Reader* (Harmondsworth: Penguin, 1977); while the source of Karl Marx's statement is *Marx and Engels on Religion* (Moscow: Progress Publishers, 1975). Blaise Pascal's penetrating and yet pithy sayings are found in *Pensées* (Harmondsworth: Penguin, 1966). The works of three authors mentioned in this chapter are of outstanding significance in relation to Christian apologetics: I refer to Albert Camus, whose book *The Myth of Sisyphus* (Harmondsworth: Penguin, 1975) I have quoted;

Ernest Becker, whose *The Denial of Death* (New York/London: The Free Press/MacMillan, 1973) and *The Structure of Evil* (New York/London: The Free Press MacMillan, 1968) are quite brilliant; and the founder of the school of Logotherapy, Viktor Frankl, whose *Man's Search for Meaning* (Boston: Beacon Press, 1964) is referred to in this chapter. Peter Berger's *Facing up to Modernity* (New York: Basic Books, 1977), while clearly sociological in approach, was highly suggestive for Christians sensing the need for a theological critique of contemporary culture.

The other sources used in this chapter are Jacques Ellul, *Hope in Time of Abandonment* (New York: Seabury Press, 1977); Klaus Bockmuehl, *The Challenge of Marxism* (Leicester: IVP, 1980); and Douglas John Hall's superb treatment of the doctrine of humanity, *Imaging God – Dominion or Stewardship* (Grand Rapids: Eerdmans, 1986).

Chapter Six

The quotation from Paul Tillich comes from a sermon entitled 'Behold, I am Doing a New Thing' in *The Shaking of the Foundations* (Harmondsworth: Penguin, 1962). Anna's struggle for faith is recounted by Arnold Bennett in a chapter entitled 'The Revival' in *Anna of the Five Towns* (London: Methuen, 1925). The poem 'The Chapel' is from the collection *R.S. Thomas – Selected Poems* (London: J.M. Dent, 1996) and is used with the kind permission of the publishers. Another volume of this poet's work strongly recommended is *No Truce with the Furies* (Newcastle-upon-Tyne: Bloodaxe Books, 1995). I regret that the source of David Mills' statement on the condition of Anglicanism has been misplaced; it articulates the perspective on that tradition held within the Reform movement in the Church of England. The comments of Michael Riddell on New Zealand and the crisis facing Christendom in general are from his *Threshold of the Future: Reforming the Church in the Post-Christian West* (London: SPCK, 1998). Klaus Bockmuehl's words are from 'Secularisation and Secularism: Some Christian Considerations' in *Evangelical*

Review of Theology, 1986, 10/1:50–73. The extended quotation from David Wells will be found in his *No Place for Truth or, What Happened to Evangelical Theology* (Leicester: IVP, 1993). Peter Berger's *The Noise of Solemn Assemblies* has been mentioned above. William Storrar's comments on the situation in Scotland were taken from a lecture delivered in the University of Aberdeen under the title 'The Decline of the Kirk'. This was later published under the title 'Understanding the Silent Disruption' in *Theology in Scotland*, 1977, Occasional Paper 2: 21–36. I refer to Dave Tomlinson and John Drane and have in mind respectively their books *The Post-Evangelical* (London: SPCK, 1998) and *Faith in a Changing Culture* (London: Marshall Pickering, 1994). Various responses to Tomlinson can be found in *The Post-Evangelical Debate* (London: SPCK, 1997) and there is further discussion of this subject in David Hillborn's *Picking up the Pieces: Can Evangelicals Adapt to Contemporary Culture?* (London: Hodder & Stoughton, 1997). Robert Warren has published a great deal on this subject; my quotation here is from his 'Evangelical Learning in the Decade of Evangelism' in *Anvil*, 1996, 13/1: 7–19. Finally, Robert Dunlop's statement regarding Ireland is from his article 'Culture and the Church in Ireland' in *Journal of the Irish Christian Study Centre* 3 (1986) 11–26.

Finally, readers who wish to explore the issues dealt with in this book at greater depth may be helped by the following titles. David Lyon is a rare animal, a respected sociologist who is a committed Christian. His little volume *Postmodernity* (Buckingham: Open University Press, 1994) provides an excellent introduction to the study of contemporary, Western culture. I have recently read Leszek Kolakowski's *Modernity on Endless Trial* (Chicago/London: University of Chicago Press, 1990) and wish I had discovered it earlier. His discussions of modernity, barbarism and the dangerous philosophical and moral vacuums existing in our time are penetrating, informative and disturbing. Two other recent publications exploring the contemporary religious situation from philosophical and sociological angles are Paul Heelas (ed.) *Religion, Modernity and Postmodernity* (Oxford: Blackwell, 1998) and Jacques Derrida and Gianni Vattimo (eds.)

Religion (Cambridge: Polity Press, 1998). The first of these books is comprehensive both in its range of coverage and in the diversity of views presented and it includes a very important chapter on Pentecostalism in Latin America by Bernice Martin. The second volume is eloquent testimony to the fact that, with the erosion of modernity, religion is back on the philosophical agenda both because of its unforeseen resurgence around the world and because of the acknowledged moral and existential crises that arise when God is declared to be dead.

The following volumes are written from a range of theological perspectives but Evangelicals can find much of help in all of them: Lawrence Osborn, *Restoring the Vision: The Gospel and Modern Culture* (London: Mowbray, 1995); Jurgen Moltmann, *God for a Secular Society: The Public Relevance of Theology* (London: SCM Press, 1999); Andrew Walker, *Telling the Story: Gospel Mission and Culture* (London: SPCK, 1996); and Kenneth Leach, *The Sky is Red: Discerning the Signs of the Times* (London: Darton Longman and Todd, 1997). I must also mention an article which came to hand as this chapter was being prepared and seems to me to point the way toward an understanding of the Gospel which is refreshingly comprehensive, consistently biblical and articulates it in a manner that is contextually relevant in the situation decribed in the foregoing pages. I refer to Robert Heppe's 'The Gospel, Sanctification and Mission' in the journal published by the British Evangelical Council, *Foundations,* 1999/Spring: 3–10. Finally, three very helpful volumes written by Christians engaging in the apologetic and missionary task at the end of the twentieth century in ways that are both creative and faithful are: Timothy Philips and Dennis Okholm (eds.), *Christian Apologetics in the Postmodern World* (Downers Grove: IVP, 1995); J. Richard Middleton and Brian Walsh, *Truth is Stranger than it Used to Be: Biblical Faith in a Postmodern Age* (London: SPCK, 1995); and a brilliant analysis of Western culture from someone writing from outside of it, Vinoth Ramachandra's *Gods that Fail: Modern Idolatry and Christian Mission* (Carlisle: Paternoster Press, 1996).